A Matter of Trust:
The Guide to Gestational Surrogacy

Gail Dutton

Clouds Publishing, Irvine, California 1997

A Matter of Trust

The Guide to Gestational Surrogacy

by Gail Dutton

Published by:

Clouds Publishing

5319 University Drive, #348

Irvine, CA 92612-2935 U.S.A.

All rights reserved. No part of this book may be reproduced or transmitted in any form or by any means, electronic or mechanical, including photocopying, recording or by any information storage and retrieval system without written permission from the author, except for the inclusion of brief quotations in a review.

Copyright 1997

by Gail Dutton

Library of Congress Catalog Card Number 96-93105

Dutton, Gail

    A Matter of Trust: The Guide to Gestational Surrogacy / by Gail Dutton

        Includes bibliographical references and index

        ISBN 0-9655966-0-5

        Parenting, Medicine

Table of Contents

Foreword

1. Our Story..1
2. The Medical Procedure.......................11
3. Ethical Considerations.........................42
4. Surrogacy and the Law........................58
5. Choosing a Fertility Clinic..................84
6. Demographics of Surrogates, Surrogate Couples and the Children....................95
7. Finding and Choosing a Surrogate Program and a Surrogate......................105
8. The Contract..126
9. Expenses and Logistics.......................133
10. Managing Expectations.......................151
11. Ending the Relationship......................165

Appendix A – Web Sites and Searches...........171

Appendix B – Other Resources.......................179

Appendix C – Surrogate Agencies..................181

Appendix D – States Mandating Coverage of Infertility.................................185

Appendix E – The Court Order........................187

Appendix F – Fertility Related Medications...........193

Appendix G – Glossary....................................199

Bibliography..207

Index..218

Warning – Disclaimer

This book is designed to provide information on the subject matter covered and is sold with the understanding that the publisher and author are not engaged in rendering legal, medical or other professional services. If legal, medical or other professional expertise is required, seek the services of a competent professional in that field.

The purpose of this book is to augment information available on the topic, not to reprint all known knowledge or opinion on the topic. Read other materials in addition to this book and learn as much as possible about the topic before embarking upon the medical procedures and before forming a surrogacy relationship of any kind.

The process of gestational surrogacy may be emotionally and financially taxing. This is a relatively new field, and many aspects of it have not been adequately explored. The industry is largely unregulated, and laws and codes of conduct still are emerging and changing.

Every effort has been made to make this book as complete and accurate as possible. However, there may be mistakes, both typographical and in content. Therefore, use this text only as a general guide and not as the ultimate source of information. Seek the services of qualified professionals. Additionally, this book contains information on gestational surrogacy up to the time of printing.

The purpose of this book is to educate. The author and Clouds Publishing shall have neither liability nor responsibility to any person or entity with respect to any loss or damage caused or alleged to be caused, directly or indirectly, by the information contained in this book.

Acknowledgments

This book would not have been possible without the many experts who graciously volunteered their expertise and their time. I extend my special thanks to Dr. David Nelson at the Huntington Reproductive Center in Pasadena, CA and Dr. Michael Kamrava at West Coast Infertility & Reproductive Associates in Beverly Hills, CA for their help with the medical procedures section of this book. For her legal expertise and updates on U.S. surrogacy laws, I thank Nanette Elster at the Chicago-Kent College of Law at Illinois Institute of Technology. Invaluable advice and insights were provided by Cristie Montgomery, director of Surrogate Parenting Services in Laguna Hills, CA and Shirley Zager, director of the Organization of Parents Through Surrogacy in Wheeling, IL. Your help throughout this process has been invaluable.

I also thank my husband, Randy, for his insistence that I write this book, his constant encouragement and his culinary skills. To Scott and Sean, our sons, thank you for your patience and your hugs.

Introduction

Surrogacy is not for the faint-hearted. It is a unique and seemingly bizarre partnership that demands placing an inordinate amount of trust in a stranger who soon will know many of the most intimate details of your life, your hopes and fears and even your family's medical history. It can be inconvenient and painful for the surrogate and the couple.

The surrogate/couple relationship usually is smooth, and the overwhelming majority of surrogacy arrangements proceed quietly and happily. Only the few horror stories usually make the newspapers. Even the best situations, however, can be emotionally tiring simply because of the nature of the arrangement and medical procedures. It can be difficult to watch another woman carrying your child and, for a surrogate, to maintain some detachment for the new life growing within her. There are so many uncertainties, not only with the relationship between the surrogate and the prospective parents, but also with the laws and the medical process. There can be many setbacks and dashed hopes. Family pressures, particularly from those who don't understand or condone the process, can be disconcerting to all involved. Participating in a surrogacy arrangement takes great confidence and great patience.

When my husband and I began searching for information about surrogate parenting in late 1991, very little information was available and most of that was outdated. Since then, numerous books have been written about surrogacy. The overwhelming majority, however, deal with the issue as a societal concern, and so concentrate upon the ethics of allowing or disallowing surrogacy, correlations to adoption or prostitution, religious views of surrogacy and infertility treatments and the legal issues that surround specific — and usually infamous — surrogacy cases. A few discuss actual surrogacy situations from the 1980s. Although many of these books are interesting from a broad, sociological perspective, they provide little current information for persons who are considering entering into a surrogacy agreement today.

Medical procedures, laws, expectations and social views regarding surrogacy are constantly evolving. Even the experts who routinely deal with surrogacy may overlook some aspects and forget to provide information that may make this process easier for you. In our case, despite working with a world-renown fertility specialist and an established, professional program, details were overlooked. We learned as we went.

The situation has improved since 1992, and more information is available, but much of that is in medical textbooks and research papers. Practical information for couples contemplating surrogacy remains in short supply.

This book could be entitled, "Things I Wish I'd Known." It is a practical guide to surrogacy in a sea of evolving procedures and changing laws and ethical concerns. But, most of all, it is a chart of what to expect from someone who has been there. We had one of the best surrogacy programs in the U.S. and some of the most experienced fertility specialists in the world, and now have healthy, happy twin boys. The process is not easy, however, and there are many pitfalls. The process is detail-intensive and requires much forethought, planning and patience to run smoothly. I hope the information contained here will help other couples navigate this new, changing, territory with ease, assurance and wonderful results.

Best wishes.

1 Our Story

Unlike most couples who contract with surrogates to carry their children, neither I nor my husband had undergone infertility treatments. The cause for my inability to carry a child was clear and irrevocable. My mother battled various forms of cancer throughout much of her adult life and died of cancer at age 65. When my gynecologist found pre-cancerous cells throughout my uterus he recommended a hysterectomy. I was 31 years old. My doctor removed only my uterus, leaving my ovaries intact. I still could produce eggs.

One and one-half years later I married a wonderful man who, I knew, would become an equally wonderful daddy. He knew my medical history and was interested in exploring the possibility of surrogacy. For us, surrogacy was the best choice, allowing us to use in vitro fertilization and embryo transfer technology to have the family we would have had if I had been able to carry a pregnancy. Our children are related to each of us.

To begin, we talked to my gynecologist about surrogacy, asked for his recommendation of a surrogacy program and read articles that were appearing in our local newspapers. We interviewed two agencies in our part of the county and chose the newer of the two, based largely upon the enthusiasm of the owner. My husband and I worked closely with her to find the right surrogate for us. This is a mutual process in which the prospective surrogate can reject the couple as easily as the couple can reject her. We heard about several women throughout a six week period and agreed to meet one. As it turned out, a few days after agreeing to work together, pressures from her extended family caused her to change her mind about becoming a surrogate. After another several weeks had passed, we met a second surrogate and her husband and children, and we agreed to work together. So far, the process had taken four months.

The young lady who became our surrogate had some medical training and I was a science and technology writer, so we each were familiar with current medical recommendations, and we each took a very practical view of the process. The relationship we formed could be termed "easy-going." I trusted her judgment regarding the care of our children, whom she was carrying, and she knew that. She, in turn, went out of her way to learn about twin pregnancies. It was a good partnership. I really couldn't have hoped for anyone nicer or more willing to help. We were able to pool our knowledge and make decisions that we each were happy with. She was very easy to work with, and for that I thank her.

She and I began the process by attending separate appointments at a world-renown fertility clinic where we were given medications to help our menstrual cycles to match. While I was taking medications to enhance my fertility, she was taking medications to prepare her body to accept the pre-embryos that would be implanted. Meanwhile, we bought life insurance policies and, pending acceptance, a health insurance policy for our surrogate.

My husband and I met with our attorney and asked him to draw up our wills to account for this change in our familial status. He was unwilling to begin until the pre-embryos were actually implanted. By that time, they would not have been protected if we had died. About six weeks after the actual implantation, he mailed us draft copies of our wills. Find an attorney you trust to write your wills and insist that they be in your possession before the embryo transfer is performed.

After a round of fertility treatments to enable me to produce multiple eggs for harvesting, 17 eggs were removed for fertilization, allowing the physician to choose those pre-embryos most likely to implant for the first attempt at a transfer. About three weeks after the pre-embryo transfer, the health insurance plan we had purchased for our surrogate denied coverage because of a very minor pre-existing condition. There was a backup health plan, however, through her husband's employer.

We were fortunate and pregnancy was achieved with the first embryo transfer. (Four were implanted at once. One embryo implanted and later split and formed two babies.) Some couples must undergo second attempts, using frozen embryos, even with gestational surrogates. Several of the remaining pre-embryos were unsuitable for transfer. We currently have eight pre-embryos in storage, which poses a very large ethical problem.

The pregnancy proceeded flawlessly until, at about 23 weeks into the pregnancy, the obstetrician spotted what he thought was an abnormality in the umbilical cord and asked us to visit with the staff geneticist. Our surrogate, her husband and I sat through an interview of my and my husband's genetic histories and a lengthy monologue in which the geneticist discussed abortion. The three of us decided the geneticist's fears were probably groundless. Pregnancy continued normally.

About 24 weeks into the pregnancy, the hospital we had selected for the delivery dropped out of our insurance program and we were forced to find a new hospital and, because our obstetrician was on staff only at one hospital, a new obstetrician. His replacement was well respected in his field and was on the staff of several well-known hospitals in the area, but he was not familiar with surrogacy. That was a mistake. As it happened, our surrogate and I had one appointment with him before the babies were born.

Our surrogate had experienced some slight pains during the 26th week, but the obstetrician said everything was normal. Two days later, her water broke, but there were no contractions. She phoned and my husband and I and raced to the hospital. I phoned our surrogate program, and the program coordinator joined us all at the hospital. Our new obstetrician was summoned to the hospital from a conference he was attending in a city two hours from there. He arrived and informed us that the chances that our children would survive was poor. He provided no more information than that and stalked out of the room, ignoring any questions. Because this was 13 weeks before the due date, our surrogate was transferred to another hospital with a neonatal tertiary care unit, and we were put under the care of an excellent and caring neonatal specialist. This man answered our questions and provided excellent care for our surrogate and our unborn children throughout the day.

By evening, contractions still had not begun. Our physician was trying to delay them as long as possible to give our children as much time in uterine as possible. At that early stage, every day helped. We decided to walk to the hospital cafeteria for dinner and, of course, contractions began. When we returned, we were told to wait in the hallway during the physician's examinations. We weren't there long. Soon, she was being rushed into surgery. An emergency Cesarean section was required, because Scott – the smallest of the two babies — had gone into fetal distress. He would not survive a vaginal birth, but was in position to begin the trip through the birth canal. Our surrogate's husband was allowed to accompany her into surgery and to stay with her throughout the procedure.

By 9:30 p.m., the evening before Thanksgiving, both of our children were born alive and our dear surrogate was recovering. Birth weights were 2 pounds 1.5 ounces and 2 pounds 3 ounces. They each measured 13 inches. Our surrogate and her husband saw them in the delivery room, as they were placed into warm isolettes. Then they were wheeled to my husband and I, waiting in hallway between the surgical suite and the neonatal intensive care unit (ICU). We were allowed to see them for a few minutes each before they were taken into the ICU.

Because they were born so prematurely, we did not yet have the court order necessary in California for our babies to be listed under our last name during their hospital stay. They were born the evening before Thanksgiving, so nearly everyone who needed to sign the papers was already on holiday. The hospital, however, delayed issuing birth certificates until we received the court order. It arrived two weeks later, legally determining that my husband and I were the parents. The hospital took many more weeks to change the last names on our twin's isolettes. The rationale was that the nurses were accustomed to using our surrogate's last name to identify our babies. Although I can understand that, it was truly galling to have our children misidentified. Later, when birth certificates were issued, the information — including all names and addresses — was so scrambled it took three attempts to get it right.

Scott and Sean were in the hospital for 10 weeks, growing and learning to breath. Oddly, the three physicians attending our children never met with us. Our information about our children's health was gleaned from reading their medical charts and from conversations with the nurses. We also learned our way through the hospital's bureaucracy, as we met and phoned the hospital often regarding their health, payment plans, insurance and birth certificates.

Those 10 weeks of hospitalization were filled with daily hospital visits as we gradually were allowed to touch them, to take them from their isolettes and hold them for a few minutes and, after many weeks, to feed them from tiny, 50 ml bottles. During that time, we learned infant CPR, how to respond to apnea and how to prepare their medicines, as well as the more usual diapering, bathing and feeding skills.

Between the time Scott and Sean were born and the time they were released from the hospital we stayed in touch with our surrogate program coordinator and, to some extent, with our surrogate. About one month before the boys came home, our surrogate arranged a baby shower for us in our home. It was a wonderful thing for her to do, and allowed our friends to celebrate with us, see our baby pictures and meet our surrogate and the coordinator of the surrogate program who had herself once been a surrogate.

When our boys reached 4.5 pounds they came home, attached to apnea monitors that would alert us if either of them ceased to breathe. When the alarm sounded, we would sit them up and tap them on their backs to help them start breathing again. There were several middle-of-the-night dashes to their room. Gradually, the bouts of apnea ceased.

Our surrogate and her husband and children visited us twice after the birth, once with the surrogate program coordinator. We have pictures of each of us holding these babies and of us together. The last time I saw our surrogate was about six months after Scott and Sean were born. We invited her and her family to our house for lunch. She again offered to carry another pregnancy for us. I have only the highest of praise for her. I know that many other surrogates and couples feel as we do. Although we are no longer in contact, the bond formed cannot be broken.

After the birth, we noticed discrepancies in the bills from our fertility clinic for cryopreserving our pre-embryos. The numbers of pre-embryos fluctuated slightly, both up and down. I believe the fluctuation was merely the result of poor record-keeping because the number changes were smaller than the number typically transferred, but I never will be certain. That, like surrogacy, is a matter of trust. The cryobank that now houses our pre-embryos has confirmed the number in storage in terms of "straws"— the housing units for the embryos before implantation. Such discrepancies are rare among infertility clinics, even though they remain unregulated.

Today, as I write this, my boys are nearly four years old. They had no permanent ill effects of their premature birth. They developed their first colds at 15 months and are healthy, happy, normal little boys. Happily, our surrogate came through with flying colors. She and her husband have another child of their own. We have been truly blessed.

Timeline

A look at our timeline shows that some steps in the overall surrogacy process were out of their proper order, despite logical reasons at the time. This reiterates that surrogacy is a relationship based upon trust.

Our timeline

12/06/91 — Signed contract with surrogate program.

12/27/91 — Met infertility specialist for first time.

1/23/91 — First examination by infertility specialist. Twice each week afterwards I returned for an examination of my ovaries and a blood test for estrogen and progestrogen levels.

8 A Matter of Trust

1/24/92 — Agreed to meet and interview a potential surrogate.

1/31/92 — Met potential surrogate, her husband and children. Agreed to work together.

2/2/92 — Surrogate changed mind and dropped out of program.

2/4/92 — Menstrual cycle began.

2/11/92 — Medication taken to disrupt cycle.

3/27/92 — Met second surrogate and agreed to work together.

4/9/92 — Found health insurance plan for surrogate, faxed surrogate's information to infertility specialist.

4/21/92 — Blood test.

4/22/92 — Invited surrogate and her husband to our home for dinner.

4/23/92 — Surrogate began regular visits to infertility specialist. I begin taking Norlutate.

4/28/92 — Surrogate undergoes a physical exam.

5/15/92 — I cease taking Norlutate and begin taking Lupron.

5/18/92 — I begin taking Pergonal. Surrogate takes a pregnancy test.

5/19/92 — Surrogate signs surrogacy agreement.

5/24/92 — Ultrasound shows 10 follicles. Aspiration planned for 5/31.

5/28/92 — Ultrasound shows 18 follicles.

5/29/92 — Pick up material for the HCG shot, which will release the eggs.

6/1/92 — Aspirate eggs.

The Guide to Gestational Surrogacy 9

6/3/92 — Transfer four embryos to surrogate. Begin routine visits to infertility specialist, every two weeks for ultrasound examination of surrogate.

6/17/92 — Pregnancy confirmed.

6/30/92 — Insurance company rejected surrogate for a minor health reason.

7/2/92 — Two heartbeats were seen on ultrasound.

7/9/92 — Program coordinator and Daddy-to-be came to ultrasound to see the heartbeats on ultrasound.

7/30/92 — Eight weeks post-conception. We were released to an obstetrician.

8/24/92 — Saw obstetrician for first time.

10/30/92 — Week 21.5. Met with genetic counselor at counselor's request.

11/1/92 — Our chosen hospital discontinued its affiliation with our insurer.

11/16/92 — We interviewed a new obstetrician.

11/25/92 — Our twin babies were born at 27 weeks.

2/3/93 — Scott and Sean came home.

It seems obvious, but, don't bother with the routine examinations until you have a surrogate and a signed contract. Do not begin the process until the surrogate has passed her physical exam and you have seen the results yourselves and you have a signed contract in hand. Be willing to wait to begin treatments until she is accepted by a health insurance plan or expect to pay prenatal and hospitalization expenses yourselves. Have your wills made early.

Your program coordinator should attend to many of those details and ensure that the process proceeds in an orderly fashion. Many things are happening at once, and tests are being scheduled with several different specialists for several different people. Be patient and wait until everything is in order before proceeding to the next step. It is very easy to be caught up in the excitement of the moment and to proceed with only oral assurances. Don't.

2 The Medical Procedure

In the 1980s, the only type of surrogate arrangements people knew much about involved donor eggs. In those situations the surrogate provided her own eggs for artificial insemination, using the sperm from the prospective father. There was a genetic link to the father, but not to his wife. This is now called traditional surrogacy. In those instances, the wife is required to adopt the child in order to be accorded parental rights. Because this is a step-parent adoption, the adoption is a straight-forward process in most states, according to the Organization of Parents Through Surrogacy (OPTS).

By the early 1990s, in vitro fertilization and embryo transfer using the father's sperm and the mother's eggs was possible. This ensures that the surrogate has no genetic ties to the fetus she carries. The baby that develops is related genetically to the couple who will raise it. Genetically, the child is the same as it would have been if its mother could have carried it in her own womb. Children born in this way, using surrogate carriers, have no genetic link to the surrogate. A court order may be used to identify the legal parents, but adoption is unnecessary in most U.S. states. This approach is called gestational surrogacy or host surrogacy. Another approach to gestational surrogacy includes a surrogate and a separate egg donor as well as the woman who will raise the child. This is a less common, but viable, option and raises some legal issues regarding the mother's identity because there are three possible mothers.

Medical Overview

There are many possible treatments for infertility, depending upon its specific cause. By the time surrogacy is considered, those options typically will have failed. Surrogacy should be considered as a possible alternative for couples who cannot conceive a child or carry it safely to term. That includes women with uterine disease or other uterine abnormalities, unexplained infertility, immunologic factors that won't allow the mother to carry the child, women with severe endometriosis and those who have undergone hysterectomies. In the ideal surrogacy situation, the genetic mother's eggs are collected and fertilized in the laboratory with the sperm of the genetic father in a process called in vitro fertilization (IVF). In the U.S. in 1993, there were a total of 31,718 IVF treatment cycles. The pre-embryos that result from IVF are then transferred to a surrogate uterus.

IVF treatments for 1994 resulted in success rates in which 23.4 percent of the embryo transfers resulted in deliveries and in which 18.2 percent of the IVF cycles resulted in deliveries, based upon results from the 249 infertility clinics that reported their results to the Society for Assisted Reproductive Technology (SART). That is a significant improvement from the years 1985 to 1993, in which only 14.7 percent of the treatments resulted in live births, according to SART. Results vary among clinics.

With gestational surrogacy, only 64 clinics reported 1994 results to SART. Of the 219 cycles initiated, 85.5 percent progressed to oocyte retrieval and, of those, 97.9 percent resulted in pre-embryo transfers. The clinical pregnancy rate was 27.8 percent per initiated cycle and 33.1 percent for embryo transfer. Of the clinical pregnancies, 91.8 percent delivered. The rate of births was 67.2 percent singletons, 27.3 percent twins, 5.5 percent triplets and no quadruplets, SART reported.

Another option is an oocyte donation program, in which eggs are donated to those couples who have a high risk of passing on hereditary genetic defects or who cannot produce eggs in sufficient numbers or of sufficient quality to be inseminated. Some physicians also will advise oocyte donation because of the age of the woman, rather than infertility. Although the infertile mother may carry these eggs, a gestational surrogate may be used when that is not medically possible. You may or may not meet the donor or be given her name, depending upon the program and the logistics involved, but you will have a detailed profile of the donor that includes her personal and medical history, family medical history and a photo.

Testing will be extensive while physicians are trying to diagnose the reason for infertility. Once surrogacy is chosen, however, the process becomes relatively straightforward. The prospective mother can expect blood tests to determine whether she has the required levels of certain hormones that are essential for reproduction and the husbands can expect to undergo a semen analysis to determine the numbers, concentration, shape (morphology) and active movement (motility) of his sperm. The woman also can expect a series of ultrasound examinations to check the development and size of her ovaries and follicles.

The Regimen

Once a surrogate is selected (and medically and psychologically approved), either the surrogate or the prospective mother will begin a series of medications designed to synchronize their reproductive By doing this, the physician ensures that eggs can be taken from the prospective mother, fertilized and implanted at the optimum times, causing as little disturbance as possible — at least for the embryos — in life's natural rhythms.

The synchronization of reproductive cycles between the gestational surrogate and the biologic mother is accomplished through the use of various medications. One class of commonly-used medications is referred to as a gonadotropin-releasing hormone agonist (GnRH-a). The most often used GnRH-a is Lupron, manufactured by TAP Pharmaceuticals.

As background, the ovaries are controlled by the pituitary gland, located in the brain. The pituitary hormones that regulate the ovaries are called gonadotropins (gonad refers to the ovary and trophic means to nourish) and include follicle-stimulating hormone (FSH) and luteninizing hormone (LH). When the ovaries are stimulated by FSH and LH, the produce the hormones estrogen and progesterone. Those two hormones stimulate the uterus to grow a lush lining — the endometrium — that serves as an ideal environment for embryo implantation. Until Lupron was developed, that complex series of endocrinologic events was extremely difficult to synchronize between women.

Lupron acts at the pituitary level to selectively stop the outflow of FSH and LH. When these hormones are stopped, the ovaries become dormant, waiting for a hormanal signal to tell them what to do. Because of that inactivity, the ovaries cannot produce estrogen and women develop menopausal-like symptoms that include hot flashes and vaginal dryness. Also, the uterine lining cannot be produced. As a result, the uterus also is dormant. Your experiences with Lupron now provide a very good idea of how your body will respond when it enters menopause.

Lupron is administered as a subcutaneous injection in the fatty tissue of the thigh. The needles are short and thin, similar to those used for insulin injections. The injection itself feels like a pin prick. These injections continue, generally, for between 7 and 14 days, although it sometimes takes longer to take effect. Because the Lupron must be refrigerated, you should choose a set time each day to be home for the shot. If you must be away, stay near a refrigerator or pack some ice until you can return the medication to its usual storage place.

Some fertility clinics use norethindrone tablets, manufactured by ESI Lederle Inc. and called Aygestin, to modify the standard Lupron protocol. This drug is a small pill, about the size of a birth control pill.

About 7 to 14 days later, the mom-to-be begins daily hip injections of human menopausal gonadoptropin (HMG), to stimulate follicle formation and maturation. The most common HMGs are Pergonal, by Serono Laboratories; Metrodin, also by Serono; and Humegon, by Organon Pharmaceuticals. Dosage is calibrated to each woman's individual response.

Potential side effects of HMG include temporary swelling of the ovaries, associated pelvic pain, pressure, weight gain and swelling. A complete list of side effects is included in Appendix G. The side effects usually resolve themselves with rest without sexual intercourse, or just after the next menstruation. Expect the injection sites to be sore and, possibly, red. There also is the possibility — still debated in the medical literature — that HCG may increase a woman's risk of developing ovarian cancer. Be aware that these are not the only follicle stimulating drugs available. For example, clomiphene citrate, manufactured as Serophene by Serono and as Clomid by Marion Merrell Dow, was introduced in the 1950s with great success, despite side effects that have included blurred vision, ovarian cysts, ovarian enlargement, throbbing, hot flashes, insomnia and irritability. It is still available. Talk with your physician about the effectiveness, expense and availability of the possible medications before you begin a drug regimen.

Injections of Humegon, Pergonal or Metrodin begin with the confirmation that the Lupron injections are effective. They frequently begin at the onset of menses. Effectiveness is determined by assessing the blood estrogen levels and by ultrasound examinations of the ovaries. Once HMG injections begin, expect an exam about every two days. Injections typically are given for 7 to 12 days. Metrodin and Pergonal are both hip injections. The drugs themselves are tablets that must be reconstituted with sodium chloride. You probably will need your husband or a friend to administer these shots each day. Some people can administer these injections themselves, but they tend to be nurses or other medical professionals who are experienced with giving shots to others and deal well with the pain of receiving these shots.

You will be shown how to do these injections at the fertility clinic and told to practice on an orange. (It's amazing how well an orange mimics the feel of a human body!) The needles are 1.5 inches long and are thick. The first set of injections, naturally, is the worst. It doesn't seem possible that there is so much space between the top layer of skin and its destination, especially when you can reach back and feel the cartilage beneath the skin. Don't worry. Even the tiniest women have enough thickness in that area to accept the needle easily. Unless your husband is a pro with injections, he probably will be nervous, too, and may feel some guilt at the pain the shots are causing you.

Every woman I talk with admitted that the shots of Pergonal and Metrodin hurt. How much varied, but by the end, we all said we felt like pin cushions. I flinch easily, so my pre-shot a hot, relaxing shower. Then I would lie on the bathroom carpet to minimize the distance I could travel during each flinch for the two slow injections. Each woman I talked with was sore, bruised and bloated. Anecdotal reports indicate that Humegon is less painful..

During the course of the injections you will visit the fertility clinic about twice each week for a blood test to check your estrogen level — which determines when the follicles will release the eggs — and for an ultrasound, to monitor the development of the follicles for their size and their readiness to release eggs. A follicle length of at least 18 mm is considered a good size. About 84 percent of the eggs extracted from the larger follicles will be mature, and will be surrounded by a complex of cells called cumulus moss. On an ultrasound, the ovaries with follicles look like potatoes that have started sprouting. About 12 days after the HMG injections begin, you can expect the eggs to be aspirated (removed) vaginally and fertilized. This time will vary slightly for every woman. Thirty-six hours before the aspiration, you will give yourself a shot of human chorionic gonadotropin (hCG), in the hip to release the eggs. The hCG replaces the lutenizing hormone surge that would normally trigger ovulation, letting the physicians determine the best time for egg retrieval.

While the prospective mother is taking medications to stimulate egg maturation, the surrogate also is taking hormones to prepare her body for pregnancy. Estrogen, taken either as a pill daily or as shots twice each week continue for several weeks to help ensure that the lining of the uterus (the endometrium) can accept the embryo once it is implanted. Then, when the eggs are aspirated from the mom-to-be, the surrogate begins taking progesterone.

The clinic may forget to tell you until the last appointment before the eggs are aspirated and fertilized, but the prospective father should have no ejaculations for at least two days before the in vitro fertilization, but shouldn't go more than four days without ejaculating, and some experts say no longer than seven days without ejaculating. That time frame ensures the highest sperm count and the best quality sperm — just what you want for baby-making.

The day of the egg aspiration, you need to arrive with your husband or his sperm. The sperm should be as fresh as possible, and clinics generally recommend that it arrive no later than one hour after ejaculation — the point after which sperm begins to die. Carry it in either a sterile glass jar or a plastic specimen cup. Keep this sample at body temperature to prolong its freshness. Because sperm must be kept somewhat warm and are extremely sensitive to time lags outside the body, it's usually better to produce the sperm contribution at the clinic rather than producing it at home and carrying it with you. If you choose to produce it elsewhere and carry it to the clinic, confirm the time of the appointment and that the clinic and its laboratory will actually be open at that hour. Keep the jar of semen near your body, as close to body temperature as possible. Many women carry it inside their blouses or let it rest between their legs enroute to the clinic. Men can put it underneath their underarms. (A note: 250 million sperm still don't qualify you to use the carpool lane.) If you choose to produce your sperm at the clinic, ask if it has a room designated for that purpose.

Once the fertility clinic has the sperm, it will be washed to prepare it to fertilize the egg. Surprisingly, sperm don't leave the body ready to fertilize an egg. Instead they remove themselves from the semen in the cervix and discard a cap-like covering from their heads in the female genital tract. To simulate this process the sperm are separated from the semen in the laboratory, leaving the sperm more active, and the covering is removed from their heads in a process called capacitation. Then the sperm are immersed in another liquid to await the arrival of the eggs.

The actual egg aspiration occurs in a surgical suite with the patient receiving either a general anesthetic or a paracervical block. Some women need no anesthesia. For the aspiration, ultrasound is used to guide a needle and catheter to the follicles on the ovaries. The needle punctures the follicle and sucks the eggs into the needle, through a catheter lined with Teflon to reduce turbulence that could damage the eggs, and into a warm test tube. About 90 percent of the eggs can be collected. This is an outpatient procedure and you can go home shortly afterwards. You may be slightly sore, and there are risk associated with any surgical procedure, but this procedure is nothing to fear.

After aspiration, the eggs may be placed in another solution for a few hours if they need to mature further before they are mixed with sperm. About four hours after the aspiration, the eggs and sperm will be put into the same solution so fertilization can occur. About 50,000 sperm per egg per dish, on average, will be added to the solution containing the eggs. The actual numbers of sperm will vary from about 10,000 to 500,000 per egg per dish. This mixture is then placed in an incubator to allow fertilization to occur. If the clinic has determined that the sperm will be unable to penetrate the eggs, the fertility specialist may inject a single sperm directly into the egg, holding the egg with a very fine pipette while another pipette that is about the thickness of a human hair is used to inject the sperm through a slit that has been created in the egg's outer membrane. The fertilized eggs will be examined about 18 hours afterwards, to ensure that they have two pronuclei (the nucleus of the sperm and the nucleus of egg, just before they join to form the one nucleus of the zygote — the fertilized egg). If more than two pronuclei have formed 17 to 20 hours after fertilization, the pre-embryos have an 87 percent chance of having chromosomal abnormalities that will cause the fetus to die or that will cause the baby to die shortly after birth. In comparison, eggs with only two pronuclei have a 29 percent chance of having chromosomal abnormalities, according to Carl Wood and Alan Trounson in the 1989 book, **Clinical In Vitro Fertilization**. Since that book was published, other studies have shown a significantly higher rate of chromosomal abnormalities, depending upon the age of the female, according to David Nelson, M.D., Huntington Reproductive Center. If the semen is normal, there is a 70 to 80 percent fertilization rate. Fertility clinics indicate that about 90 percent of all patients undergoing this procedure actually proceed to the next stage: pre-embryo transfer.

Pre-Embryo Transfer

Generally, pre-embryos are transferred two days after the eggs are fertilized. The West Coast Infertility & Reproductive Associates in Beverly Hills, CA is pioneering a new method in which the pre-embryos are allowed to grow in solution for five days before they are implanted. According to clinic director Michael M. Kamrava, M.D., this method offers better natural selection and improves the pregnancy rate because it allows the physicians to select the viable embryos with greater accuracy. He said it also decreases the rate of higher order multiple pregnancies. The rate of tubal pregnancies also decreases because the pre-embryos are more closely matched with the time and stage of development of the endometrial growth. Additionally, "If the earlier developing pre-embryos do not make it to the firth day, they are the ones that would have not made it in utero either, and the couple need not be given false hopes of pregnancy and the two weeks of anticipation," he said. "So far, we have used this technique in 21 patients and we have had, approximately, a 50 percent pregnancy rate from this group," he added.

Pre-embryo transfer is like an insemination except that embryos are being injected, rather than sperm. Typically, between three and four embryos will be drawn into a catheter (a small tube), which will be inserted through the surrogate's cervix and into her uterus, and then discharged. Whether and where an embryo implants depends both upon the quality of the embryo and the quality of the endometrium within the uterus.

Most physicians use four embryos at a time, but the actual number will vary among clinics. In 1996, one California fertility specialist implanted seven embryos. Five of those attached and were born. Typically, between 20 and 40 percent of the women who become pregnant using infertility drugs will carry multiples.

Some fertility researchers, however, have reported that increasing the numbers of pre-embryos transferred together has no effect upon the number of embryos that actually implant, suggesting that implanting one embryo is as effective as four. That view is a minority opinion, however, and requires additional testing. When commenting upon the use of natural cycle ovulation retrieval in in vitro fertilization (NORIF), Dr. Kamrava told the **Los Angeles Times** that, "The success rate so far seems to be close to the rate for traditional IVF. With NORIF, we are running a 15 to 17 percent pregnancy rate." He did not comment on the delivery rate, however.

The goal is to have one, or maybe two, embryos implant in the uterus. Having three or more embryos that actually implant into the uterus is considered dangerous to the health of the surrogate and to that of the developing babies. This concern may cause a specialist to remove the embryo that is the smallest or that is in the least advantageous position within the uterus — a case of the one sacrificing all for the good of the many. The procedure, called selective reduction, is performed only with the patient's approval and involves injecting potassium chloride into the fetus in the least beneficial position in the uterus, causing it to die immediately. Unfortunately, the procedure also is risky for the remaining embryos and risks inducing the miscarriage of all of the remaining embryos.

The American Society for Reproductive Medicine is considering developing the first guidelines to limit the number of embryos transferred to a uterus to four for women age 34 and younger, but to allow higher numbers for older women, who are less likely to become pregnant. Those guidelines are most likely to apply to the age of the egg donor.

The actual embryo transfer to the surrogate takes about five minutes to complete, but the surrogate usually is required to stay at the clinic for one to four hours, laying on her back. There are reports that some medical facilities do not require any bed rest after implantation. Then, after returning home, she usually is asked to spend the next two to three days lying on her back to help increase the changes that a fertilized egg will attach itself to her uterine wall. She also will be expected to avoid any heavy lifting, stress, vigorous exercise or anything that could raise her body temperature and prevent the embryos from attaching. She will continue taking the series of hip injections of progesteron, forfive to eight weeks after the transplant, depending upon her response.

Multiple Births

Multiples (twins, triplets, etc.) occur about one 20 to 40 percent of the time with in vitro fertilization procedures, but not all can be carried to term. Twins are the most common multiples, with about 125 million in the world. In the U.S. in 1987, nearly 82,000 twins and other multiples were born. According to the National Center for Health Statistics, the rate of higher order multiple births (three or more babies) increased 113 percent among Caucasian mothers in a comparison of data collected in studies conducted in 1972-1974 and 1985-1989 and by 22 percent in the same comparison of black mothers. There were particularly large increases in multiples born to mothers aged 30-34 years (152 percent), mothers aged 35-39 (165 percent) and mothers aged 40-44 (123 percent). Much of the increase was attributed to infertility treatments and an upward shift in mothers' ages. Twins were not included in the study, but of higher-order multiple births, 90.4 percent were triplets, 8.4 percent were quadruplets and 1.4 percent were quintuplets. Although the mortality of higher order multiples was about 15 times that of singletons, infant mortality among higher orders multiples declined by about 50 percent between 1960 and 1985.

Twins and higher order multiples are more likely to be conceived by older, heavier and taller women. The Yoruba tribe in Nigeria has the highest incidence of multiples in the world — 45 of 1,000 births, according to Elizabeth Nobel, author of the book **Having Twins**. She also wrote that the Chinese and Japanese have the lowest incidence — 4 per 1,000 births. Multiples are most likely to be born of mothers whose birthdays are between January and May, who also had mothers born in the winter, and the probability of a twin birth is highest in November and lowest in May, according to studies in Italy and England, respectively.

Cryopreservation

If the couple wishes, any remaining, viable, embryos that were not transferred may be frozen (cryopreserved) at about -80 degrees Celsius or lower for later possible implantation, thus providing a second set in case the first attempt fails or in case the couple decides to have another child. This method of preserving human embryos first succeeded in 1983 in the Netherlands, and resulted in identical twin girls. It was followed, one year later, with a birth in England. Before this live, offspring from frozen pre-embryos had only been born to cows, rabbits, sheep, rats, goats, horses, antelopes and baboons.

Pre-embryos may be frozen (cryopreserved) at any one of three stages:

- Pronucleate embryos are frozen as one cell the day after they are inseminated. When thawed, they should have clear cytoplasm (the substance between the cell's wall and the cell's nucleus), intact zona pellucide (shells), and be capable of cleaving after an overnight culture.
- Early cleavage embryos are cryopreserved two to three days after insemination. Upon thawing, at least half of their blastomers (cells) should be viable and the zona pellucide should be intact. These embryos usually are transferred the same day they are thawed.
- Blastocysts are preserved at an expanded stage. Upon thawing, they should re-expand after an overnight culture. Blastocytes can attach to the uterus wall and have a central cavity and an outer cell layer that will provide nutrients for the growing cells.

Before the pre-embryos are frozen they are exposed to cryopreservatives that help them to survive the freezing and thawing process. The two broad classes of cryopreservatives are permeating and non-permeating, and are chosen based upon the stage of embryo development at the time of freezing and upon the specific properties of the cryoprotectant, including toxicity and permeability. Either of these cryoprotectants typically are added to the solution containing the pre-embryos while the pre-embryos are at room temperature, in increasing concentrations. Then the pre-embryos are loaded into the straws or vials in which they will undergo freezing.

Cryopreservation involves forming ice crystals in the medium in which the cells — pre-embryos — are contained without causing ice to form within the cells themselves. The cells are cooled slowly, at a rate of about 3 degrees Celsius per minute. At temperatures of -5 to -7 degrees Celsius, the medium containing the pre-embryos is seeded by hand. That process involves touching the straw or vial with a pair of tweezers that have been pre-cooled in liquid nitrogen, in an effort to control the freezing process and so prevent spontaneous freezing, which could kill the pre-embryos. These ice crystals cannot cross the cellular membrane of the pre-embryos. The buffered salt media and cryopreservatives in which the pre-embryos are stored helps the water to leave the cells through osmosis, gradually dehydrating the cells and preventing ice from forming within the cells from their own liquid. Once the temperature plummets to -35 to -110 degrees Celsius, the straws or vials holding the pre-embryos are inserted into liquid nitrogen for long-term storage.

The length of time pre-embryos can be stored is open to debate. Theoretically, they should survive cryopreservation indefinitely. In practice, fertility programs tend to limit storage to 6 to 10 years.

Once the embryos are thawed, the cryoprotectants are removed from the solution in a series of gradual dilutions that causes the cells to shrink and swell, thus risking cellular damage. Successful pregnancies can results from those pre-embryos, but fertility specialists tend to wait up to one day after the thawing to observe the cells and ensure that they are dividing properly before implanting them in the uterus.

Another cryopreservation method, called vitrification, uses high concentrations of permeating cryoprotectants. After exposure, the container of pre-embryos is plunged into liquid nitrogen for a very fast freezing that turns the liquid within the cells into a non-crystalline, glass-like solid, eliminating the risk of intracellular ice forming.

The percentages of embryos surviving freezing and thawing vary widely. SART's figures for 1994 indicate that 96 percent of the thaws resulted in transfer, but that the rate of deliveries per thaw was only 15 percent and that deliveries per transfer procedure was only 15.6 percent. The survival rate after a thaw has improved substantially since 1989 when survival rates for cryopreserved embryos typically were 60 to 75 percent and pregnancy rates were 12.5 percent for cryopreserved pre-embryos.

The rate of survival after freezing depends largely upon the quality of the pre-embryo and the quality of the pre-embryo when it was frozen. Among early cleavage embryos, those frozen two to three days after fertilization, the rate of survival is inversely proportional to the number of cells present in the pre-embryos when they were frozen. Results in 1992 from St. Mary's Hospital and the Manchester Fertility Services, both in Manchester, England, indicate a 67 percent and 66 percent survival rate of pronucleate (one-celled) and early cleavage embryos, respectively. Among blastocysts, about half of the individual cells do not survive the freeze/thaw process, so blastocyst cryopreservation rarely is offered.

As an example, in 1985 at Bourn Hall Clinic, 261 couples began frozen embryo transfers there, and 230 (85%) actually had embryos suitable for transfer. Of those, (81%) had viable pregnancies, but only (26%) delivered babies or had pregnancies in at least the 28th gestational week. Clearly, cryopreserved embryos have a lower implantation rate than fresh embryos.

Live birth rates, using the Manchester data mentioned earlier, indicate a 14.2 percent rate with pronucleat embryos and an 11.8 percent rate with early cleavage embryos. Results were slightly better for women using their natural cycle than for those using hormone replacement therapy. In the United Kingdom overall, the live birth rate is 10.7 percent for cyropreserved embryos.

Worldwide, in 1990, there were 23,865 embryos frozen, up from 14,657 in 1988, according to the book, **Children of Choice**. Also in 1990, 3,290 frozen embryos were thawed and implanted, resulting in 382 pregnancies and 291 live births. Since then, these numbers have increased substantially.

Data from Bourn Hall, Cambridge, U.K., indicates that the rate of congenital abnormality in humans is the same for cryopreserved embryos as for those human embryos that were conceived naturally.

Animal research reported in the February 1995 issue of New Scientist, however, indicates that cryopreservation causes subtle changes in behavior or physiology that are undetectable at birth but may become apparent later in life. In animal studies conducted by Emmanuel Dulioust at the University of Paris XI, male mice of a particular strain (B6CBA) that were born after cryopreservation and implantation had an 11 percent weight gain between their 39th and 67th weeks of life, compared to a mere 2.4 percent weight gain for mice born via IVF without cryopreservation. Females from that same strain who were born from cryopreserved embryos performed more poorly in tests of exploratory behavior than did female mice from the same strain who had not been cryopreserved as embryos. However, when mice from another strain (C3D2) were tested, the cryopreserved mice performed better than their never-frozen counterparts. There is speculation that the effects of cryopreservation may be more pronounced in longer-lived species, such as humans.

Storage

The infertility center either will store extra cryopreserved pre-embryos itself or will transfer the pre-embryos to a cryopreservation facility. A few days before the eggs are aspirated and the pre-embryos are formed, the infertility center will have the couple fill out a form describing their wishes for their disposition of any extra pre-embryos. Depending upon the center, the form may be a simple checklist listing three options (storage for later implantation, donation to another couple or use as research), the fee and the period of cryopreservation, or may be a multipage document that stipulates their management and disposal in virtually any eventuality, including the death of the husband, wife or both; their separation; the attainment of a certain age; and the abandonment of the pre-embryos. It also may stipulate whether the couple has the right to change their minds regarding embryo disposition and whether they will be notified before the embryo disposition.

What may not be addressed is what happens to the pre-embryos if the fertility center ceases operation or how the pre-embryos will be protected from such disasters as fire, flood, earthquake, electrical failure or other natural or man-made disaster. If the center ceases operation, the pre-embryos should be transferred to another cyrobank in that area and the clients should be notified of the transfer and provided with the bank's name, director, address and phone number. Once notified, the couple should ascertain the bank's fees and policies, including whether it needs a new disposition form for its files. It is a good idea to check the number of pre-embryos the new bank says it received and to attempt to resolve any discrepancies.

No facility can be completely safe from disaster, but it may be worthwhile to assure yourselves that adequate protection is in place for the more routine hazards. For example, does the clinic have an automatic, emergency power generator to maintain power to the refrigeration system? Can the storage vault withstand fire or a power outage? Are the pre-embryos protected from fire?

Prenatal Care

Once pregnancy is determined — about two weeks after the embryo transfer — visits to the fertility clinic for the surrogate will occur weekly. Once a heartbeat is documented and appropriate growth is shown, the surrogate normally is released to an obstetrician. If the surrogate is carrying multiple babies, however, the fertility specialist is likely to continue seeing the surrogate for a few more weeks. In my case (a relatively rare situation in which a single embryo implanted and divided into two embryos after being implanted, thus creating identical twins) the first heartbeat was seen on ultrasound July 2 — one month after implantation — and reconfirmed July 9. We were released to an obstetrician in mid-August.

Success Rates

Even with a healthy fertile couple, the odds of a naturally occurring pregnancy are slim when you consider that there are about 200 million follicles in the human ovary at birth that can eventually form, and that in 35 years of menstruation only about 400 would develop to a point allowing them to be fertilized.

Female fertility peaks by age 25 and falls throughout the remainder of her reproductive life. Yona Tadir, medical director at the Beckman Laser Institute at the University of California at Irvine, reports that, "During IVF, seven or eight out of ten eggs will be fertilized if the sperm is of normal quality and only two or three will implant in the uterus and develop into a normal pregnancy. Those numbers go down when either sperm or eggs have other problems."

With a fertility clinic, successes and failures are amplified, because you are aware of each step of the process. Success rates, measured by live births as well as by pregnancies, vary significantly from clinic to clinic as well as from couple to couple, based upon the medical condition of the prospective parents and their ages, as well as the age and condition of their surrogate. When you compare clinic success rates, be certain you are comparing the same things. Some clinics measure live births, others measure pregnancies that enter the second trimester, others measure clinical pregnancies.

Among women over age 40, in-vitro fertilization results in pregnancy about 15 percent of the time. That's an 85 percent failure rate. Of those 15 percent, however, between one-third and one-half will miscarry. That means that, for women over the age of 40 undergoing in vitro fertilization in which they also are the carrier, they go home with a baby about 8 percent of the time. In comparison, only about 15 to 20 percent of all normal pregnancies end in miscarriages. Data from the Center for Surrogate Parenting in Beverly Hills, California, indicates that the 26 percent miscarriage rate for gestational surrogates in its program between 1986 and 1993 was similar to the miscarriage rate for women over age 35 in the general population. However, the overall success rate for gestational surrogates was higher than the overall IVF rate.

Boosting Fertility

There are ways to improve the quality of the eggs and sperm, which the couple should embark upon as early as possible before IVF begins. Sperm has a three month development cycle, so your diet and lifestyle today has far-reaching consequences. To help ensure healthy sperm and a healthy baby:

- Stop smoking and avoid cigarette smoke as much as possible. Men who smoke have about 22 percent less sperm in semen samples than do men who don't smoke. The by-products of cigarette smoke reduce the sperm count, speed and size by 20 percent, according to a 1995 study in the Archives of Andrology. People in a very smoky room for one hour are estimated to inhale the equivalent of smoking 10 to 15 cigarettes. Additionally, the rate of miscarriages increases 64 percent when both partners smoke, or when just the man smokes.

- Quit drinking alcohol. Fathers who routinely drank two drinks per day or five drinks at one sitting had babies that were 6.5 ounces smaller than other babies, regardless of whether the mother smoked or drank. Additionally, alcohol lowers the sperm count as well as the potency of the sperm that are produced. The reason is that drinking impairs liver function, allowing female hormones to accumulate and eventually interfere with sperm production.

- Keep your scrotum cool by wearing boxer shorts and, if you exercise intensely, reduce the intensity of your regimen.

- Avoid excessive hot tub usage.

- Protect yourself, to the extent possible, from environmental chemicals. Learn which chemicals you contact. Some can cause reduced sperm counts or abnormal sperm, increasing the risk of birth defects. The same is true of X-rays.

- Eat a balanced diet. This means diets based upon pure water, fresh fruits and vegetables, whole grains, low-fat protein like skinless chicken, fish and legumes. There is some evidence that a balanced diet — even before pregnancy — can affect the health of the baby. For example folic acid is necessary for the synthesis of DNA and other nutrients (specifically the L-carnitine – not the D- or DL- form of carnitine) enhance sperm production and speed. In the case of IVF and surrogacy, there is a chance that a balanced diet may help preserve the integrity of the eggs and produce healthier sperm.

- Quit using illicit drugs, including marijuana. Long-term use of marijuana lowers sperm counts and causes sperm to develop abnormally.

- Increase the percentage of antioxidants in the diet. Specifically, vitamin E, coenzyme Q10, selenium, zinc and glutathione and other antioxidants improve sperm speed and density.

- Increase your vitamin C intake. Low levels of vitamin C cause sperm to clump together and is the cause of infertility in about 16 percent of men.

- If a low sperm count is a concern, try to time the IVF procedure so that the sperm and eggs are united between February and March. Studies have shown that most men have a reproductive rhythm, with the highest sperm counts of the year occurring in February and March, and the lowest sperm counts occurring in September. Unrelated studies conducted by Harry Fisch, M.D., director of the Male Reproductive Center, Department of Urology, Columbia-Presbyterian Medical Center in New York, also found seasonal fluctuations in sperm counts that he suggested influence the seasonal fluctuation in birth rates.

- Abstain from sex for two to seven days before the eggs are inseminated, to increase the volume and motility of the semen. (Experts disagree on the actual length of time. Check with your physician.)

Male infertility can be caused by numerous factors, including:

- Structural damage to the reproductive system.
- The use of anabolic steroids.
- The antidiarrheal drug sulfasalazine.
- The antifungal medication ketoconazole.
- A drug to treat ulcerative collitis, azulfidine.
- Varicocele (a vericose vein in the testicle).
- Infections diseases in adulthood, including mumps.
- Fevers.
- Tuberculosis.
- Chemotherapy.
- Excessive stress.

For what it's worth, sperm counts have risen significantly since 1970, according to Dr. Harry Fisch. In his study of 1,283 men who banked semen before undergoing vasectomies between 1970 and 1994 in New York, Los Angeles and Roseville, MN, the average sperm concentrations increased from 77 million to 89 million sperm per milliliter of semen. No change in motility or semen volume was noted. However, there was a significant geographic variance in the concentration. Men in New York City averaged 131.5 million sperm per milliliter while those in Roseville, MN had 100.8 million sperm per milliliter and those in Los Angeles had 72.7 million sperm per milliliter.

Male Infertility

About 35 percent of the time – some studies say up to 50 percent of the time – infertility is a male problem. The most common reason is a low sperm count, although many other causes are possible, including impotence and ejaculation disorders.

Harvard University scientist A.P. McMahon and colleagues in March 1996 reported that the Desert hedgehog (Dhh) gene is essential to male fertility. If there is a complete absence of mature sperm, the Dhh gene may not be present. Ontogeny, Inc., a biotech firm in Cambridge, MA, is developing hedgehog-based pharmaceuticals to treat male infertility, but that was in animal trials in 1996. Before a medication can be commercialized it must progress to large mammal studies and then through three phases of human trials before final data can be submitted to the Food and Drug Administration (FDA) for review and possible approval. Therefore, commercialization is not expected for several more years.

Other research at the University of Pennsylvania's School of Veterinary Medicine have succeeded in transplanting testicular tissue from one mouse into another, causing the recipient mouse to produce the donor's sperm. For humans, this means that males eventually may be able to bank their own tissue before undergoing chemotherapy or other procedures that could threaten fertility. It would allow tissue from one man to be transplanted to another, thus causing the recipient to produce sperm with the genetic code of the tissue donor. Compared to freezing the sperm themselves, freezing tissue sections offers the advantages of routine handling procedures and the availability of all of the individuals potential gene combinations.

Fisch had no explanation for those differences, but they could be caused by variations in physical activity, the propensity to use hot tubs or the ethnic makeup of the men.

Other studies have reported decreases in sperm counts, but Fisch suggested that geographic variability may account for the reported decline. "Earlier studies were from the United States, particularly from New York, where sperm counts are the highest. In contrast, later studies were from areas that were not represented earlier and included several studies from third world countries where sperm counts were low," he explained. When the earlier studies were reanalyzed, Fisch found they supported his findings.

Risks of IVF

Some early, unconfirmed, studies have indicated that treatments with fertility drugs may increase a woman's risk of developing cancer. Hyperstimulation of the ovaries is a documented risk. And, about 15 percent of the women undergoing IVF never have eggs retrieved because they do not product eggs of sufficient maturity.

The risks to the children born through IVF seem to be no greater than for normal conceptions and births. For example, only about three percent of the 23,000 "high-tech" babies born in the U.S. since 1978 (when the first child was born in the U.K.) had birth defects. That figure is comparable to the risk for the general population. There are some concerns that techniques that select the sperm may allow sperm with some chromosomal damage to fertilize eggs and cause the birth of children who, as adults, will have infertility problems of their own. That possibility relates to the long-held theory that the fittest sperm impregnates the egg. However, other scientists maintain that fertilization is more of a chance encounter of egg and sperm than a race to the finish line, and so believe that natural selection has little role in pregnancy at this level. Recent research from Belgium, which maintains the largest registry of IVF babies, suggests this technique has no higher incidence of birth defects or chromosomal abnormalities than other methods of fertilization. That was confirmed December 1996 by Cornell University researchers.

There is, however, a 20 to 40 percent chance that multiple babies will be born because of the number of embryos implanted into the uterus. With that comes what is termed a "high risk" pregnancy and the likelihood that twins or triplets will be born prematurely and will still need to grow and develop. Typically, twins are born six weeks early and may require a few weeks of hospitalization. They also may be born late in the second trimester and can survive and become healthy children. However, they probably will be unable to breath without assistance, suck, swallow or perform the other skills expected of newborns, and will have very low birth weights. Very premature babies also may have a range of problems that affecting the heart, lungs, brain, and eyes. Death, blindness, brain damage and learning disorders are among the complications.

A test currently is being developed to determine an individual's risk of premature delivery. Researcher Roger Smith and his team at the John Hunter Hospital in Newcastle, Australia found that the amount of a chemical that the placenta begins to secrete early in the second trimester, called corticotropin releasing hormone (CRH), is a fairly accurate predictor of premature births. At 16 to 20 weeks into a normal 40 week gestation period, Smith and his team measured the CRH levels in 485 women and compared them to actual birth dates for their children. The 24 women who delivered prematurely (before the 37th week) had an average of 3.64 times more CRH in their blood than those who delivered on time. Those who delivered late had less CRH. Although the role of CRH is largely unknown, it seems that its concentration in the blood rises dramatically as the delivery date approaches. More tests will be conducted to determine its role in pregnancy and labor.

Depending upon your insurance coverage, providing the intensive care needed by these children may significantly affect your finances. Naturally, the earlier multiples are born, the greater the hospitalization costs and the length of hospitalization. Although prices and medical practices vary widely throughout the U.S., expenses in excess of $250,000 per child for 10 weeks of hospitalization, beginning with the neonatal intensive care unit and progressing to the usual nursery for newborns, are to be expected. Even if your insurer pays 80 percent of the expenses, the bill for ICU care for multiples is significant.

Science Update

In vitro fertilization (IVF) has come a long way since the first "test tube baby" was born in 1978. A series of new methods, including using lasers and tiny needles to help the sperm penetrate the egg, as well as special nutrient-rich coatings for the fertilized egg, are helping the process along. Some of those procedures risk damaging the chromosomes or the possibility of fertilizing an egg with an abnormal sperm. Work to minimize that possibility is still underway. Some of the newer techniques follow.

NORIF

Natural Cycle Ovulation Retrieval in In vitro Fertilization (NORIF). This methods relies upon the natural ovulation cycle, with no hormonal stimulation. The patient goes to the fertility clinic a few hours before egg release is likely, so the fertility specialist can retrieve and fertilize the egg. Generally, up to two eggs are produced. The benefit is that it costs about one quarter of what a traditional IVF (in vitro fertilization) course costs, no general anesthesia is required and there are no side effects (from the hormones used for IVF). Pregnancy rates vary with the clinic and with the age of the woman. Another advantage is the lack of hormonal stimulation, thus minimizing the health risk and discomfort, and the lack of extra pre-embryos, which allows a couple to avoid a very difficult ethical question.

Sperm Sorting

Although it is possible to use sperm sorting for sex selection, it currently is used prevent passing sex-related diseases to offspring. For example, a woman who carried the gene for hydrocephalus — a disease that causes fluid to accumulate in the cranium — used this method to select a female embryo to carry, thus virtually guaranteeing that her child would not develop hydrocephalus, which usually affects only males. The process involved staining the sperm with fluorescent dye and reading it with a laser beam. Sperm that carries the female X chromosome is brighter than sperm that carries the male Y chromosome. Sorting is 90 percent accurate, according to the U.S. Department of Agriculture researcher who developed this technique

Percutaneous Epididymal Sperm Aspiration (PESA)

Designed for some patients who have undergone vasectomies, lack a vas deferens, cannot ejaculate or have occlusions of the epididymus, percutaneous epididymal sperm aspiration offers a minimally invasive way to obtain sperm for IVF. Either a light intravenous sedative and/or local anesthesia is used, and the man may return to work the same day. To obtain the sperm, the testicle is held so it cannot move while a needle, connected to a syringe is inserted. As the needle is withdrawn, suction is applied to the syringe to withdraw fluid that then is inspected for sperm.

Intracytoplasmic Sperm Injection

With intracytoplasmic sperm injection (ICSI), a single sperm is injected directly into the cytoplasm of the egg. This procedure, developed by the Center of Reproductive Medicine in Belgium, requires a minimum number of sperm and offers a higher success rate than other treatments for male factor infertility. Recent research at the Center and at Cornell University has shown that this method does not increase the rate of birth defects.

Sperm Placement

Dr. Tadir at the University of California at Irvine's Beckman Laser Institute is developing ways to manipulate sperm using a laser "tractor beam." As this beam passes through a cell, it is bent, exerting a small force that can hold a swimming sperm immobile. This may one day be used to drag sperm into contact with an egg cell.

Microembryonic Hatching

After in vitro fertilization — but not after natural fertilization — the microembryonic shell (the zona pellucida) hardens. Microembryonic hatching counteracts this hardening by creating a small hole in that shell that allows the microembryos to release easier into the endometrial cavity and to make it easier for the embryo to hatch from that shell and implant in the uterus. The practice has increased pregnancy rates in some studies.

Oocyte Cryopreservation

Research also is underway to allow eggs to be frozen, eliminating the need to produce excess embryos for eventual freezing. Currently, about 40 percent of the eggs that are frozen until needed and then thawed can be fertilized, compared with about 60 percent of fresh, never frozen eggs and 90 percent of frozen sperm. In freezing eggs, Debra Gook, PhD, at the Royal Women's Hospital in Melbourne, Australia began working with Ricardo Asch, M.D., then at the UCI (University of California at Irvine) Medical Center. Dr. Gook's process uses a slow-freeze, fast-thaw technique to preserve the eggs. This involves coating the eggs with protective chemicals and freezing them with liquid nitrogen for 90 minutes, until they reach -30 degrees Celsius and them rapidly chilling them to -150 degrees Celsius in about 20 minutes. The next, highly controversial, step is to determine whether these frozen eggs will consistently develop into normal embryos.

Ovary Cryopreservation

In late 1995 it became possible in animals to remove and cryopreserve a slice of ovarian tissue and reimplant it, allowing that tissue to begin producing eggs. This treatment remains investigational and as of January 1997 had not been attempted in humans. First introduced at the Genetics & IVF Institute in Fairfax, Virginia, in collaboration with Dr. Roger Gosden in Great Britain, this therapy may be particularly useful before a woman undergoes chemotherapy or other fertility-threatening treatments.

With it, one ovary is removed via laproscopic surgery. The section of the ovary that contains the eggs is sectioned into thin tissue slices and cryopreserved. Then after chemotherapy is completed and the oncologist feels fertility may be a medically appropriate option, the ovarian tissue slices can be thawed and reimplanted into the ovarian bed. The ovary will begin functioning normally after a few months and, in animal models, has produced normal offspring. The procedure remains in early stage human trials and, so far, no data is available.

3   Ethical Considerations

The ethics of surrogacy are a flash point. The debates question the rightness of IVF treatments as well as the even more controversial involvement of gestational surrogates. Depending upon the source, the objections include a belief that medical interventions are wrong, that the separation of sex from procreation is immoral, that surrogacy implies that women have value primarily through their ability to bear children, that the process is somehow dishonest because the chances of bringing home a baby are rather slim, because it may harm some pre-embryos, because it involves a third party in procreation and because it may harm the sanctity of marriage.

By 1994, more than 40,000 children worldwide had been born thanks to in vitro fertilization. None-the-less, it remains a cause of concern in many countries, primarily because of such associated issues as embryo preservation, wastage, embryo and gamete donation and surrogacy. In random surveys conducted in Japan and New Zealand in the early 1990s, people viewed the benefits of IVF — and science in general — in humanitarian terms rather than economic, but the Japanese perceived more benefit from the field of genetic engineering than from IVF. The New Zealanders, conversely, perceived more benefit from IVF than from genetic engineering. Of those surveyed, 61 percent of the Japanese were most concerned about IVF. An earlier study, conducted in 1985 by the Japanese Prime Minister's Office indicated that 29 percent approved of IVF for humans and 55 percent disapproved. By 1990, 30 percent approved and 49 percent disapproved of IVF. In the situation of married couples who can have children no other way, a 1984 survey of Japanese housewives indicated that 62 percent approved the use of IVF. More recently, 41 percent of women undergoing infertility treatments indicated they would consider gestational surrogacy, compared to 18 percent who would consider traditional surrogacy.

In New Zealand in 1984 — before gestational surrogacy was possible — 88 percent of respondents (from a pool of 1,400 people) indicated that they favored IVF for married couples. And only 8 percent were against IVF.

What is a Mother?

Some people, cultures and religions believe that surrogacy somehow alters and confuses familial ties for the couple and for any children born through surrogacy. The growth of surrogacy leads some to ask, "Who is the real mother?" Because of surrogacy, it is possible that two — or in cases using donor eggs — even three women could legitimately claim to be the mother. So, the question becomes, "What is a mother?" Does providing the genetic material to create a baby make a woman a mother? What about carrying a child and giving birth? Or, is it the intent to care for and nurture a child that makes a woman a mother? The contention throughout the ages that the mother is woman who gave birth to a child — and who, until relatively recently also was the genetic mother and was usually the person to nurture the child — is being questioned in light of the technological advances that have made gestational surrogacy possible. Arguments favoring the gestational carrier as mother state that the carrier has invested more of herself in this child than has the genetic mother. Anyone who has undergone infertility treatments might challenge that assumption.

There is a broad assumption, generally based upon adoption situations, that the "real" mother is the mother who intends to nurture the child after its birth. Much of the literature concerning surrogacy also mentions the "right to raise a child". Some go as far as to say that this "right" should not be dependent upon the ability to conceive, carry or bear a child. Talk of a "right" to raise a child in this context seems to be over-reaching, but there is a constitutional right to privacy. It is logical to then believe that privacy also extends to a couple's decision to have a child by natural or assisted reproductive techniques or by adoption. The medical community views infertility as a technical problem with a technical solution. Value judgments and talk of rights are not an issue.

The next logical question is, "What is a family?" In the case of gestational surrogacy, what is the surrogate's role? In some surrogate contracts today, all contact between the surrogate, the couple and the child ceases shortly after the child's birth. In other contracts, the surrogate merely may agree not to try to form a parent-child relationship. Also, the parties generally agree to maintain the privacy of the situation and to not disclose the identities of the others involved in the contract and, sometimes, even the existence of a surrogacy arrangement. In practice, close friends and family almost always know the details of the arrangement and sometimes even the identities of the people involved. The child also should be told.

Keeping this in mind, there has been no declared intent to form a blended family that includes the surrogate, her family, the couple, their families and the child born through surrogacy. This intent — or lack thereof — is important, at least psychologically because it allows the couple and their child to establish a traditional family, just as if the child had been carried by the genetic mother, and allows the surrogate to proceed with her own life without engendering ties and responsibilities to another family in whom she might otherwise have no great interest.

Commercial Surrogacy

Becoming a surrogate is a personal choice and many believe that to deny women the right to use their unique capabilities in carrying a child for another couple is to treat women as lesser citizens — ones who are not fully responsible for their decisions and who are not sufficiently rational to make those decisions. That reasoning, however, leads to the contention that many of life's major contracts are invalid. If we knowing how we will feel in the future is required for informed consent, "People would never be deemed competent to decide about their will, their medical treatments, their marriages, even about the decision to become parents or not become parents," according to Christine Sistare who is quoted in the book, **The Criminalization of a Woman's Body**.

One of the big issues is whether surrogates should be paid for their services. A few states, including Michigan, New York, Utah and Virginia, have banned paid surrogacy. Other states have laws against baby-selling and do not differentiate between gestational surrogacy and other forms and maintain that the surrogacy contract, regardless of how it is written, is a contract for the sale of a child. It is worth noting, however, that gamete and sperm donors receive payment and that adoption agencies allow the adopting parents to pay the expenses of the birth mother. This may become the prevailing norm for surrogacy because states with surrogacy laws often base them upon adoption laws.

With this in mind, surrogacy contracts tend to be worded so that payment to the surrogate is for a variety of expenses related to the pregnancy and to her well-being during the pregnancy. This distinction also affects income taxes. If a surrogate were paid for services, the expectant parents would be responsible for paying employment taxes (Social Security, FICA, and worker's compensation) just as if they had hired a secretary or a nanny. The surrogate then would have to pay federal withholding taxes. Expense reimbursements, however, are non-taxable. Regardless of the wording you use, money is never exchanged for an actual child. Therefore, the genetic parents pay the surrogate's expenses (all related medical expenses, travel and other specified items if legal in your area) regardless of the outcome of the pregnancy.

The primary argument against paying surrogates is that payment opens the door to exploitation — especially because surrogates tend to have less formal education and lower income levels than the couples who hire them. Part of this is simply related to age. It's normal for finances to improve as one ages and gains more work experience. Conversely, many maintain that not paying surrogates is merely another form of exploitation — one that denies women one outlet for supplementing their incomes while reaping the benefits of their labor. Proponents of payment say it is a woman's right to determine what to do with her own body and that she may agree or refuse to agree her physical capabilities to help another couple conceive a child of their own. It is difficult to establish the difference between selling one's capabilities as a surrogate carrier and selling one's capabilities as a nurse or construction worker or any other job one is capable of performing.

Cryopreservation

One of the great debates — particularly for parents of children born via IVF — is the fate of frozen embryos. In the beginning, when you are hoping that many eggs will be produced and that at least one will implant, the bounty of pre-embryos is a blessing. Later, when you have a child or two in your arms and realize you still have several fertilized eggs in storage, that bounty becomes a serious ethical issue. When you feel your family is complete, does the existence of these fertilized eggs morally require you to attempt to have them implanted? Do you leave them frozen forever, thereby compelling your estate — presumably your children — or the government to determine their fate after your death? Or, is it permissible to donate those fertilized eggs to another couple, in effect, allowing another couple to raise your children? Is thawing and discarding the frozen pre-embryos tantamount to murder?

There are tens of thousands of frozen embryos stored throughout the world, and the number is growing. This single issue has raised serious ethical, legal and religious concerns that all hinge on when, exactly, life begins. If life begins at conception — defined as the union of the sperm and egg — are parents morally obligated to implant all of their embryos? The options for the couples whose sperm and eggs united to form these pre-embryos are to allow the embryos to be discarded or used for medical research, donate them to an infertile couple or to attempt to use them in the hopes of having more children themselves. That can be a daunting prospect when one considers that couple often have 8, 10 or 12 pre-embryos frozen. Many couples find this an impossible decision and so leave their pre-embryos frozen indefinitely. In making this decision, it is important to have a firm understanding of conception and of what actually has been frozen.

Conception is not instantaneous. After the sperm and egg unite, their chromosomes fuse into a single cell, which then divides during the course of the next three days to form a four-, six- or eight-celled embryo. Pre-embryos may be frozen at any point after they form one cell until they become blastocysts (Chapter 2). Importantly, however, simply transferring embryos does not mean a woman is pregnant. The embryos must develop to the blastocyst stage, in which the fertilized egg has a central cavity surrounded by an outer cellular layer that will developed into the trophoblastic (feeding) layer that eventually will become a placenta. At the blastocyst stage, the embryo is capable of attaching to the uterine wall. Once the embryo implants itself into the wall, pregnancy begins. When the fertilized egg implants, the inner mass of cells that will become the actual embryo have not yet developed. Those cells will organize into the first building blocks of an actual embryo — the embryonic axis along with the major organs and body structures will form — early in the second week after the egg is fertilized.

With this in mind, most professionals familiar with surrogacy — including scientists, legal advisors and ethicists — contend that these pre-embryos are not yet persons because before implantation they cannot develop individually and may never develop, but they are more than merely human tissue because of their ability to eventually develop into persons, given the right environment. As a result, they lack the protection giving to children and instead are accorded special respect.

Also consider the legal definition of death. In Ireland, the U.S. and the United Kingdom, irreversible cessation of all function of the entire brain, including the brain stem, constitutes brain death. At the stage at which the embryos are frozen they have not yet developed brains or circulatory systems. Therefore, the pre-embryos have not yet developed to the point at which the definition of human or animal death applies, indicating that they have not yet achieved personhood.

In the U.S., a few states ban the intentional destruction of pre-embryos. Think long and hard about these questions before you have the reality of frozen pre-embryos to deal with. Also, talk with your fertility specialist to determine whether creating an abundance of embryos is really necessary. It is possible to harvest many eggs but to only allow the most viable to be fertilized, and some fertility specialists say that under some situations, implanting one fertilized egg is as effective as implanting four. Because the latter option eliminates the need for hyperstimulating the ovaries, it costs significantly less than traditional IVF methods and is more natural.

Beyond the issue of what to do with these embryos, who "owns" them if the couple dies or divorces? What recourse is there if they are destroyed in a fire or natural disaster or if they are stolen? Those issues all are compelling and have not yet been answered definitively, although several legal cases have addressed the issue of divorce with varying outcomes.

Before the child's birth, everyone associated with the process is excited about the numbers of embryos created. They represent hope... possibilities that an infertile couple will have at least one child. The fate of the remaining pre-embryos embryos after that child or a few children are born typically is discussed only briefly. The gravity of the situation rarely is faced until the couple decides their family is complete. By then, it is too late to do anything other than rationalize the decision.

Who is Eligible

One of the first issues the medical establishment confronts is who is eligible for IVF surrogacy. In the United Kingdom the guidelines are clear-cut and closely resemble those for the United States. The main indications for surrogacy include:

- Patients with functioning ovaries but without a uterus, either because of congenital reasons or because of a hysterectomy for carcinoma, severe hemorrhage or ruptured uterus.

- Women who have had repeated miscarriages and for whom the possibility of carrying a baby to term is quite remote, as well as for those who have been unable to conceive following other assisted reproductive methods.

- Women with medical conditions that make pregnancy life-threatening but who are otherwise healthy.

Importantly surrogacy is not allowed in Great Britain as an option for those with purely social or career concerns. The U.S. does not regulate surrogacy, although a few individual U.S. states do have their own laws regarding it.

Religious Views

The religious response to surrogacy and reproductive technology is varied. The Catholic church considers IVF immoral, Lutherans have no official opinion but tend to discourage it except in certain — usually unnamed — circumstances. Noted fundamentalists ministers have denounced reproductive technology. Jewish writers argue there is a moral obligation to take any reasonable steps to preserve reproductive health, but argue that because birth endangers a woman's life, she also should have the joy of raising the child. Some of the dissent is based upon the standard arguments of the sanctity of life and the effect upon marriage, but other arguments include the possible long-term effects of the medical treatments upon the child, the risks of childbirth to the gestational surrogate or the fear that a child will replace God in a couple's hearts.

In a 1988 survey of Christian, Jewish and Muslim perspectives on reproductive technology conducted by the U.S. Office of Technology Assessment, only Christian Scientists and Reform Jews supported surrogacy. Of the 17 groups surveyed, all but three allowed IVF if it involved only spousal genetic material and no embryo wastage. Those supporting it included Anglican, Lutheran, Reformed, Methodist, Mennonite, Baptist, Evangelical, Adventist, Jehovah's Witness, Mormon, Orthodox Jewish, Conservative Jewish, Reform Jewish and Muslim groups. Those positions, however, reflect church dogma and not necessarily the beliefs or practices of the congregations.

The bulk of the decisions regarding the appropriateness of IVF or surrogacy, however, involve the methods used rather than the broad technology. For example, "Treatments that involve collecting genetic material for diagnostic purposes provoke questions about the appropriateness of masturbation and the propriety of engaging in sexual activity that cannot lead to conception," according to Arthur L. Greil, associate professor of sociology, Alfred University, Alfred, NY. All groups who have addressed the issue express great concern about the rights of the embryos. Can they be experimented upon? Must they all be implanted? Can they be destroyed? Who should look out for their well-being?

The introduction of genetic material from a third party also raises concerns, and elicits calls to ban oocyte donation, sperm donation and traditional surrogacy. Gestational surrogacy itself also elicits concerns about the introduction of a third party – the surrogate — into a marriage, and the legal and moral rights and responsibilities of that party. Depending upon the religious body — notably Catholics and fundamentalist Protestants — the use of a surrogate may be considered adultery.

Baha'i Faith

Baha'i religious law does not permit its members to engage in surrogacy. Baha'i writings indicate that the introduction of a third party into the process of procreation challenges the sanctity of marriage. Likewise, artificial insemination (AI) and other assisted reproduction technologies are accepted if they involve only the husband, his wife and their physician. For example, AI is considered acceptable as long as the husband's sperm and wife's eggs are used. If donor sperm or donor eggs are used, the practice is not acceptable.

Buddhist

The Buddhist faith does not address surrogacy. The Buddhist Churches of America, headquarters for that faith in the U.S., maintains that surrogacy is up to the individual and that the church has no policy regarding it. Its philosophy encourages preventive healthcare, but has largely avoided debates of medical ethics. To reach a conclusion regarding the issue of surrogacy and the creation of additional, unimplanted pre-embryos, individuals must determine when personhood is achieved. According to a paper published in the Journal of Buddhist Ethics by James J. Hughes at the Center for Clinical Medical Ethics, University of Chicago and Damien Keown, at Goldsmiths, University of London, "Most Buddhist commentators have adapted classical Hindu Teachings that the transmigration of consciousness occurs at conception, and therefore that all abortion incurs the karmic burden of killing. Before modern embryology...ideas about conception were scientifically inaccurate and often associated the beginning of life with events in the third or fourth month of pregnancy." There also is the argument that fetuses do not fully embody all five skandhas and so are not yet persons.

Catholic

In the March 30, 1995 Evangelium Vitae (the Gospel of Life) issued by Pope John Paul II, the encyclical puts the full force of the church behind its previous pronouncements regarding human genetics. Pope John Paul acknowledged the good that can come from prenatal diagnostic techniques, provided they are used to make early therapy possible "or even to favor a serene and informed acceptance of the child not yet born," but selective abortion to prevent the birth of children with genetic defects "...is shameful and utterly reprehensible." In surrogacy, several embryos are implanted in the uterus simultaneously, occasionally making it necessary to selectively abort a fetus to help ensure the survival of the others or the health of the surrogate. It continued, "The use of human embryos or fetuses as an object of experimentation constitutes a crime against their dignity as human beings who have a right to the same respect owed to a child once born, just as to every person."

There is dissent within the Church on this issue. In discussing the imminent destruction of some 3,000 frozen embryos at fertility clinics in Great Britain, that nation's leading Catholic prelate, Cardinal Basil Hume, said on July 31, 1996, "I believe these frozen embryos are frozen human life, but I believe they should be...allowed to die and then disposed of in a dignified manner."

Lutheran

Although the Lutheran Church in America has no official stand, its literature condemns both in vitro fertilization and surrogacy as dehumanizing. Some writings addressing IVF call for strict regulations, such as limiting IVF to married women who carry the child of their and their husbands own genetic lineages. Regarding surrogacy, the **Surrogate Motherhood** pamphlet in the **Procreation**

Ethics series of essays stops short of whole condemnation, but says that "...Christian perceptions of the significance of human procreation and its place within the marital relationship are not compatible with the basic premise of surrogate motherhood: that one could deliberately conceive and bear a child with no commitment either to the child or to its father." It continues to discuss the danger that a child — particularly for an infertile couple — "...may replace God as their center of value and meaning." In contrast, an article in the Second Opinion, published by the Park Ridge Center for the Study of Health, Faith, and Ethics lends surrogacy, and IVF "qualified support" that seeks to slow the development of this technology while allowing its use.

Islam

In a published interview in 1980 with Sheikh Jadel Haq, when he was Mufti of Egypt, the issue of surrogacy was not addressed, although treatment for infertility was strongly recommended. Artificial insemination was approved providing the sperm is from the woman's husband and has not been mixed with other sperm and that the fertilized ovum is never transferred to the uterus of an animal and then implanted to the wife's uterus. Any child resulting from other types of procedures should carry the wife's name, rather than her husband's, indicating fornication. Regarding the broader issue of infertility, "Insemination of a wife with semen taken from her husband (providing it has not been mixed with other semen) is allowed."

Judaism

Jewish law — as opposed to Israeli law — has reached no conclusion regarding the maternity of children born via gestational surrogacy. There are strong arguments on each side of the issue that affect whether the child is Jewish, as well as affecting the determination of who is the first-born and even the legitimacy of the child (and thus to potential marriage partners because children who are considered illegitimate may only marry others who are considered illegitimate). Because motherhood is both genetic and gestational, there also is an argument that a child born through surrogacy actually has two mothers.

The contention that the genetic mother is the legal mother is based upon belief that the zygote acquires an identity and parentage at the moment of conception. This is particularly important because under Jewish law a child is Jewish only if its mother is Jewish. So, if the legal mother is determined to be the genetic mother, the child will be Jewish if the genetic mother is Jewish, regardless of whether or not the surrogate is Jewish. This interpretation indicates that the mother's genetic contribution is equally as important as the father's and that parentage is determined by genetics. Because there as yet is no definitive ruling, an authority on ancient law, Rabbi Kamelhar, cautions that the child should be converted if either the surrogate or the genetic mother is not Jewish, to ensure that the child is considered Jewish.

Note that the arguments advancing the case of the genetic mother as legal mother are the same arguments used against abortion and, by implication, the destruction of any extra pre-embryos. Those pre-embryos are not yet alive but represent potential life. As such, some authorities would suspend the Sabbath to save the lives of these pre-embryos. For couples with unused pre-embryos, the alternatives are implanting them and then either raising those children or allowing them to be adopted, or donating those pre-embryos to other infertile couples to implant and raise. Neither is a particularly palatable option when more than a dozen pre-embryos may be available.

Other Halachic authorities contend that until 40 days post-conception the embryo is "water" and so when transplanted becomes a part of the recipient and takes on the recipient's identity, just as a transplanted heart becomes a part of its recipient. That argument implies that frozen embryos are not yet human because they have not yet been implanted. There is also an argument that children born of surrogates have two mothers and so cannot marry the children of either mother.

Contractually, Jewish law seems to indicate that a surrogacy contract is invalid because a person cannot transfer the title of something that does not yet exist. So, although the contract for the surrogate's services is legitimate, a new contract would need to be entered into after the child's birth — or perhaps 40 days post-conception — in order for the surrogate to be contractually bound to give the child to its genetic parents. Although no consensus has been reached, experts on Jewish law indicate that the bulk of the arguments favor the surrogate mother as the legal mother and that surrogate contracts are unenforceable.

Practical Effect

Despite the concerns raised by religious authorities throughout the world, religious leaders are having little effect upon infertile couples. In research conducted by sociologist Arthur L. Greil, "Infertile couples aren't heeding religious advice." He found "…high levels of public support for reproductive technology — sometimes as high as 90 percent for IVF and 60 percent for surrogacy. For infertile couples, practical concerns overshadow ethical concerns. Couples rejected treatment not because the next step was morally repugnant but because they were tired of the process or because they saw adoption as a faster means of realizing their goal.

"This is the first generation to come of age believing in the myth of birth control — that human reproduction can be controlled by technology." Therefore, Greil said, "Accepting the Vatican instruction's approach to infertility requires a spirit of resignation — not a common spirit among couples pursuing infertility treatment." The Vatican instruction was to "...find the occasion for other important services to the life of the human person," in one's sterility.

4 Surrogacy and the Law

Surrogacy is a relatively new legal field that redefines the terms mother, father, family and even personhood. As a result of the many questions this raises, the United States has no nationwide policy and has left it to the individual determination of its 50 states.

Although the law varies among the states, in 1994 the U.S. Supreme Court refused to hear a California case, and so let stand a decision in California that established the intended, biological, parents as the legal parents in the case of gestational surrogacy. The ruling was the final decision in the case of Anna Johnson vs. Mark and Crispina Calvert. As a result, California law maintains that the gestational surrogate has no legal, parental rights regarding any child she carries for another couple. In that particular case, the surrogate contract was deemed enforceable, thus providing sufficient legal foundation for other persons entering into surrogacy contracts to also expect their contracts to be enforceable under California law.

In California in 1992, Governor Pete Wilson vetoed a bill that would have regulated contracts with surrogate mothers. Despite the veto, the legislation remains as a sound guideline for surrogate contracts and its recommendations have been adopted by many surrogacy program coordinators in the state. The failed legislation specified that surrogates were at least age 21, had one child of their own, receive psychological counseling before an embryo was implanted and after the child's birth. It also exempted money paid to surrogates from a law that considers it a felony to sell or pay for the custody of a human being. The intended parents would be responsible for the surrogate's legal advice and health services throughout the pregnancy and, under that legislation, the surrogate would control her medical treatment and choose her health care providers.

This bill differentiated between traditional surrogates (who are the genetic mothers) and gestational surrogates (who have no genetic ties to the child), providing that children born to traditional, genetic surrogates then be adopted in a step-parent adoption by the intended mother and that children born to gestational surrogates automatically belong to their natural, genetic parents.

In vetoing that bill, California Governor Pete Wilson said, "Surrogacy is a relatively recent phenomenon. The full moral and psychological dimensions of this practice are not yet clear. In fact, they are just beginning to emerge. Only two published court opinions in California have treated this nettlesome subject. No state has adopted regulations on this matter. (sic) Comprehensive regulation of this difficult moral issue is premature in California as well. To the extent surrogacy continues to be practical, it can be governed by the legal framework already established in the family law area."

Changes made to the U.S. minimum wage law in 1996 may have an unintended effect upon surrogacy legislation. Under the law, persons adopting a child could receive a nonrefundable tax credit up to $5,000 per child to be used for "qualified" adoption expenses, plus $1,000 if a child with physical, emotional or mental handicaps was adopted. The "qualified" expenses included attorney's fees, court costs and other costs associated with the adoption. Importantly, this tax credit is not available for adoptions that result from surrogate arrangements. That exclusion seems to support the belief that the child is being adopted by its own, genetic parents and that, therefore, no incentive to adopt is necessary. According to a spokesperson for the House Ways and Means Committee, no opposition to surrogacy was voiced during discussions of this amendment, but the relationship of a parent to a child born through surrogacy was considered biological. Because of that rationale, this may be the first small – although unintended – step towards federal recognition of the rights of the genetic parents in surrogacy.

U.S. State Laws

U.S. state laws vary widely regarding surrogacy. Whether surrogacy is legal or a punishable offense depends upon the state, and the punishments range from moderate fines to imprisonment. States with legislation tend to base surrogacy upon laws relating to adoption or to child-selling, which are irrelevant when applied to gestational surrogacy.

For example, considering the fact that a husband and wife give the surrogate their genetic material for incubation until that material can be returned to them (in the form of a child), the surrogate has nothing material to sell. The situation is analogous to paying a sitter to care for children. Paying the sitter does not mean the parents bought their children back from the sitter at the end of the evening! Although the length of time the surrogate cares for the child is certainly longer and the location of the care differs, she still is providing care and nourishment for a child with different genetic parents. Most current laws ignore that fact. Many of the laws were written with little input from infertile couples or those who have been involved with surrogacy — either traditional or gestational — and so are written with an inaccurate understanding of the process. Others are written in response to notorious situations like New Jersey's Baby M case in the late 1980s.

Strong lobbies have formed on all sides of the issue. Arguments include allegations of baby-selling and the fear that children and their gestational mothers may be defined as commodities. Some detractors of surrogacy have suggested that even a gestational surrogate, who has no genetic link to the child, should not be held to a surrogacy contract because she may be incapable of knowing her true wishes regarding the child before its birth. The implication is that women cannot make rational decisions regarding reproduction and child rearing prior to the child's birth.

To date, individual U.S. states typically have been ambivalent about passing legislation. Most states simply have no precedents for surrogacy cases, causing the judges to, in effect, make new law with each decision. Often they turn to existing adoption policies as guidelines, which have little bearing upon gestational surrogacy. Opponents of surrogacy legislation argue that the existing laws are sufficient to regulate this relatively new reproductive option. None-the-less, under existing laws, the infertile couple and the surrogate could be subject to prosecution under felony and misdemeanor statutes because compensation may indicate that a child is being bought or sold. Surrogacy contracts sidestep the problem by reimbursing the surrogate for living expenses and the costs associated with the pregnancy. Other laws could cause the attorneys, physicians and others participating in the surrogacy agreement to be considered guilty of conspiracy to create a life for the purpose of sale.

Although only a few surrogacy arrangements — about one quarter of one percent — have ever been contested in court, many believe it is time for family law to catch up to modern reality. According to the Organization of Parents Through Surrogacy (OPTS), of the more than 8,000 surrogate births recorded in the U.S. between the mid-1970s and the early 1990s, including traditional and gestational surrogacy, only 17 have engaged in legal battles over custody. Of those, fewer than 10 were over physical custody, according to Shirley Zager, director of OPTS. In contrast, about 15 percent of adoptions involve legal battles over custody.

The United States clearly needs one set of regulations governing surrogacy that acknowledges the reality of gestational surrogacy and that takes into consideration the technology involved.

Many states have considered surrogacy legislation, but only a few have enacted laws regarding surrogacy.

Alabama

Alabama exempts surrogacy from statutes to prevent baby-selling and allows payment to surrogates.

Arizona

Arizona prohibits surrogacy contracts and the use of surrogacy agencies (paid intermediaries). Until 1996, Arizona law recognized the surrogate as the legal mother and her husband as the legal father and explicitly includes gestational surrogacy under these regulations. That provision of the Revised Statutes was declared unconstitutional in the case of Soos vs. Superior Court in and from the County of Maricopa.

Arkansas

Arkansas declared surrogacy legal and recognizes the biological father and his wife as the parents by court order after the child's birth.

California

California is the U.S. state most friendly to the genetic parents. Although it has no laws developed specifically for surrogate situations, a legal precedent in the Johnson v. Calvert case was codified in California Civil Code 7003 in 1993. In it, all parental rights are assigned to the genetic parents of a child born through surrogacy because the child would not exist but for the genetic parents and the intent of the genetic parents was to have a child, they acted upon their intention, going to immeasurable lengths. Their intent was not to donate a zygote. Because of the strong support in California for genetic parents, couples from throughout the world go there to enter into surrogacy agreements.

Additionally, California has proposed legislation requiring written approval of donors before human eggs, embryos or sperm can be transferred to others. Failure to obtain consent would result in physicians losing their licenses. Another bill makes it a felony to intentionally use such genetic material without written consent of the donors. After passing the state Senate in August 1996, the bills await approval from the Assembly.

District of Columbia

The District of Columbia considers surrogate contracts unenforceable. It bans surrogacy contracts and payment to any intermediary, including surrogacy programs, for matching surrogates and commissioning couples and explicitly includes gestational surrogacy in these regulations. Persons or entities involved in forming a surrogate contract for any form of remuneration are subject to a fine of up to $10,000 and one year in prison.

Florida

Florida state statutes require couples and surrogates to enter into a binding contract for gestational surrogacy. Only infertile couples may contract for gestational surrogacy. The contract is not binding unless the surrogate is at least 18 years old and unless the commissioning couple are legally married and each are at least 18 years old. Only couples with a medical reason for gestational surrogacy can enter into such a contract. The contract must stipulate that the surrogate is the sole source of consent regarding clinical intervention and management of the pregnancy, that she will submit to a reasonable medical evaluation and treatment and adhere to reasonable medical instructions regarding prenatal health and that she will relinquish all rights and responsibilities to the child unless genetic testing determines that neither member of the commissioning couple is the genetic parent of the child. Regarding reimbursement, "The commissioning couple may agree to pay only reasonable living, legal, medical, psychological and psychiatric expenses of the gestational surrogate that are directly related to prenatal, intrapartal," (birthing) "and postpartal periods."

Within three days of the birth of the child the couple must petition the court for an expedited affirmation of parental status. The court will then fix a time and place for a hearing and will provide notice to the gestational surrogate, the treating physician for the assisted reproductive technology program and any party claiming paternity. If any of those parties desire privacy, their names may be deleted from the notice of hearing and from the copy of the petition. The hearing will be held in a closed court. If at least one member of the commissioning couple is the genetic parent of the child, the commissioning couple will be presumed to be the natural parents. Within 30 days after the entry of the order, a certified statement from the state registrar of vital statistics will be filed, a new birth certificate will be issued that names the commissioning couple as parents and the original birth certificate will be sealed.

Regarding the disposition of eggs, sperm or pre-embryos, Florida stipulates that any remaining genetic material will remain under the control of the party that provided it and that the couple has joint authority regarding the pre-embryos. Unless a written agreement specifies otherwise, the genetic material shall remain under the control of the surviving member of a commissioning couple in the event of one member's death. "A child born from the material of a person or persons who died before the transfer of their eggs, sperm or pre-embryos to a woman's body shall not be eligible for a claim against the decedent's estate unless the child has been provided for by the decedent's will."

Georgia

Georgia currently has no legislation regarding surrogacy, although surrogacy is certainly a viable option there and can be accomplished with both genetic parents' names appearing upon the birth certificate if the couple has an innovative attorney. The remedy to that situation was to have been H.B. 1073, which died in committee at the end of the 1996 session. That legislation duplicated Florida's laws regarding gestational surrogacy. To receive action, the bill would have to be reintroduced.

Illinois

Illinois has no laws specifically governing surrogacy and so relies upon adoption law. Even in the case of gestational surrogacy, the genetic mother must adopt her own child in a step-parent adoption because the law assumes that the mother is the person who actually gave birth to the child. The Illinois Adoption Act allows the adoptive parents to reimburse the biological mother for medical, hospital, lodging, food and clothing expenses during the pregnancy and for no more than 30 days after the child's birth.

Indiana

Indiana code states, "It is against public policy to enforce any term of a surrogate agreement that requires a surrogate to do any of the following:

- Provide a gamete to conceive a child.
- Become pregnant.
- Consent to undergo or undergo an abortion.
- Undergo medical or psychological treatment or examination.
- Use a substance or engage in activity only in accordance with the demands of another person.
- Waive parental rights or duties to a child
- Terminate, (sic)care, custody, or control of a child.
- Consent to a stepparent adoption under IC 31-3-1."

Additionally, in the case of custody disputes, an Indiana court may not base a decision concerning the best interests of the child solely on evidence that a surrogate and another person entered into a surrogate agreement unless it can be proved that the agreement "… was entered into through duress, fraud or misrepresentation." Therefore, surrogacy is allowed, but surrogacy contracts are unenforceable. As of 1996, the only commissioning couple to lose custody of their children involved a husband who only wanted one of the twin children. The surrogate refused to allow the twins to be separated and won custody.

Iowa

Iowa exempts surrogacy agreements from baby-selling statutes and allows payments to the surrogate. As of 1996, the only reference to surrogacy in Iowa's state statutes is listed under statutes regarding kidnapping.

Kentucky

Kentucky recognizes that there are fundamental differences between surrogate parenting procedures and the buying and selling of children. Its statutes specifically do not prohibit in vitro fertilization. None-the-less, in the opinion of the Attorney General, "Neither a surrogate mother nor anyone else involved in a surrogate parent transaction may receive payments as consideration, regardless of whether the transaction is accomplished through an adoption proceeding or as a termination of parental rights proceeding..." The Notes to Decision for Kentucky Code 199.590 (Protective Services for Children – Adoption) state, "When the legislature included 'in vitro' fertilization procedures in this section while leaving out the surrogate parenting procedure, the legislature was not legislating against surrogate parenting; all that can be derived from this language is that the legislature has expressed itself about one procedure for medically assisted conception while remaining silent on others." Under these statutes for adoption proceedings, expenses related to the adoption may be submitted to the court for approval.

Louisiana

Louisiana considers surrogacy contracts void and unenforceable, but does not include penalties for involvement with such contracts.

Michigan

Michigan considers entering or helping to form a commercial surrogacy contracts a crime and defines commercial surrogacy as surrogacy in which the surrogate receives compensation that is greater than her actual expenses. The penalties for entering into or helping to form commercial surrogacy contracts call for up to five years imprisonment and a $50,000 fine for surrogate brokers and misdemeanor penalties with a fine of up to $10,000 and up to one year in prison for those entering into the contract. These penalties apply to both gestational and traditional surrogacy agreements.

Maine

Maine voids paid surrogacy contracts but allows unpaid contracts. The law maintains that the biological father has legal rights and obligations regarding the child.

Minnesota

Minnesota has no legislation regarding surrogacy, although bills have been introduced which, as of 1996, had not received hearings. That state does, however, have a Recognition of Parentage procedure that allows the genetic husband to be listed as the father on the child's birth certificate. The genetic mother may have to do a step-parent adoption to obtain parental rights.

Nebraska

Nebraska laws make surrogacy contracts void and unenforceable if compensation is involved. Non-commercial surrogacy, however, is not prohibited and bears no penalties.

Nevada

Nevada laws specifically address gestational surrogacy, allowing a married couple to enter into an enforceable contract with a surrogate. The surrogate may only be reimbursed for medical and living expenses, and the intended parents are recognized as the legal parents at the time of the child's birth.

New Hampshire

New Hampshire limits the use of gestational and traditional surrogacy to infertile couples and supports the genetic parents, noting that the child born of a surrogate is the child of the intended parents from the moment of the child's birth unless the surrogate gives notice of her intent to keep the child within 72 hours of the child's birth. New Hampshire's laws provide for court approval of surrogacy agreements before they are signed and for a home-study program for the intended parents, and medical and psychological screening for the couple and for the surrogate. If the surrogate is over age 35, genetic counseling is mandated. The surrogate may be reimbursed for medical expenses, lost wages related to the pregnancy and delivery, insurance coverage, attorney and counseling fees. The law does not permit payment to intermediaries of any kind, including surrogacy programs or agencies.

New York

New York in 1992 passed a bill that prohibited "commercial" surrogacy. That bill prohibits persons or entities knowingly requesting, accepting, receiving, paying or giving any fee, compensation or other remuneration directly or indirectly in connection with a surrogate parenting contract or inducing, arranging or assisting in arranging such a contract for compensation. The genetic parents who violate that section of the law are subject to a civil fine of up to $500. Notably, the New York law does allow surrogates to be reimbursed for such expenses as hospital and medical costs, but not for surrendering the child. Non-commercial surrogacy is legal as long as the arrangements are consistent with existing adoption laws. Gestational surrogacy is addressed specifically.

New Jersey

New Jersey bans commercial surrogacy, considering it baby-selling. The New Jersey Parentage Act holds that the mother is the woman who gave birth to the child, although a Certificate of Parentage can be issued by the court, based upon results of a blood test or a genetic test.

North Dakota

North Dakota voids surrogacy contracts but allows compensation for the surrogate mother, recognizing the surrogate as the legal mother.

Tennessee

Tennessee recognizes the intended parents as the legal parents, so adoption is unnecessary.

Texas

Texas does not address surrogacy, but does address artificial insemination, oocyte donation and embryo donation. In those cases, the child is regarded as the child of couple and not the child of the donor unless he is the husband of the inseminated woman. It seems that Texas adheres to the intent of the couples in determining parent-child relationships.

Utah

Utah does not recognize surrogacy contracts. It prohibits compensation for the surrogate and payment for a surrogate program or other intermediary, and recognizes the surrogate as the legal mother. Custody disputes are settled in the best interest of the child.

Virginia

In Virginia, surrogate contracts are unenforceable regarding payment mechanisms. Court approval is required before entering into a surrogate agreement. Generally, the gestational mother and her husband are presumed to be the parents of any child resulting from assisted conception but, after a surrogacy contract is approved by the court and entered as an order, the intended parents are the parents of any resulting child. To enter into a surrogacy contract, the court requires:

- The intended parents, the surrogate and her husband petition the circuit court of the county or city in which at least one of the parties resides, and sign the contract "...before an officer or other person authorized by law to take acknowledgments..."

- The local department of social services or welfare or a licensed childl-placing agency has conducted a home study of the intended parents, the surrogate and her husband and has filed a report of the study with the court.

- The intended parents, the surrogate and her husband are considered fit to raise a child.

- All the parties voluntarily entered into the surrogacy and contract and understand its terms, meanings and effects. Any agreement for payment of compensation is unenforceable.

- The agreement guarantees payment of reasonable medical and ancillary costs in the form of insurance, cash, escrow, bonds or other arrangements that are satisfactory to both parties, including allocation or responsibility for such costs in the event of termination of the pregnancy, termination of the contract or breach of contract.

- The surrogate is married and has had at least one live birth and bearing another child does not pose an unreasonable risk to her physical or mental health or to that of any resulting child.

- Before signing the surrogacy contract, the intended parents the surrogate and her husband have undergone physical and psychological evaluations by licensed practitioners in those fields and access to the results is provided to the court.

- The intended mother is infertile, unable to bear a child or is unable to do so without unreasonable risk to the unborn child or to her own physical or mental health.

- At least one of the intended parents is a genetic parent of any child resulting from this agreement.
- The surrogate's husband is a party to the surrogacy agreement.
- All parties have received counseling concerning the effects of the surrogacy by a qualified health care professional or social worker and a report containing conclusions about the capacity of the parties to enter into and fulfill the agreement has been filed with the court.
- "The agreement would not be substantially detrimental to the interests of any of the affected persons."

Under Virginia law, during the pregnancy, the surrogate is solely responsible for the clinical management of the pregnancy. Unless otherwise provided in the contract, the intended parents bear all court costs, counsel fees and other costs and expenses associated with the hearing, including the costs of the home study. Within seven days of the child's birth, the intended parents must file written notice with the court that the child was born within 300 days of the last performance of assisted conception. That filing must include a finding that at least one of the intended parents is the genetic parent of the resulting child. The count then will enter an order directing the State Registrar of Vital Records to issue a new birth certificate naming the intended parents as the parents of the child.

Virginia does allow fees to be paid to an attorney for legal advice and for writing a surrogate contract, but specifically prohibits surrogacy programs or any other entities from accepting compensation for recruiting surrogates or arranging surrogate contracts for gestational or traditional surrogacy.

Washington

Washington prohibits paid surrogacy, but allows a surrogate's expenses to be paid. It also prohibits payments to an intermediary, such as a surrogate program, and calls for misdemeanor penalties for violations of the law. Custody disputes are resolved in the best interests of the child. These laws apply directly to gestational surrogacy as well as to traditional surrogacy.

West Virginia

West Virginia recognizes surrogacy agreements and has specifically excluded them from laws against baby-selling, allowing payments to the surrogate.

Be aware that these laws may change, and are included here only to provide a general look at U.S. laws as of late as 1996. They are not intended as legal advice. Consult an attorney in your state for an update on the laws governing surrogacy in your state before entering a surrogacy agreement. Several states also have mandated insurers to reimburse IVF treatments. A list is included in Appendix D.

The laws in the state where the child is born will be used to identify the legal parents. So, if your surrogate visited California late in the pregnancy and gave birth there, California law would recognize the genetic parents as the legal parents. If the child was born in Virginia, the surrogate would be considered the legal parent and her name would be on the child's birth certificate. If she happened to visit Washington, D.C. and give birth there, everyone involved could face massive fines. However, the place of birth is not the only determining factor.

Where the child will be reared also is an issue if the child is born out of state. Your state of residence, where the contract was executed and where the child was born will all play a factor in the decision. As you enter into a surrogacy agreement, discuss these issues in detail with your attorney and ensure that your surrogate also discusses them with her attorney. You may, together, decide that she should avoid traveling in certain states late in her pregnancy as a matter of self-protection — and to protect the genetic parents, the surrogacy program coordinator and others involved — if the child is born prematurely.

Even though your state may not require a contract or may consider it invalid, some infertility specialists who work with surrogacy situations will ask to see a signed surrogacy contract or will insist that the parties sign a form indicating their intent to form a surrogacy agreement before the physicians will assist with surrogacy.

Laws regarding surrogacy are changing constantly. Do not assume that surrogacy is legal in your state or that surrogacy contracts are enforceable. Check with an attorney familiar with surrogacy, and with a reputable surrogacy program or infertility specialist in your area and also with your state senator's office. Your state's legislative analyst also is a good source of current information. Because surrogacy is such an emotional issue, it may be worthwhile to determine your source's position on surrogacy and check a few different sources to ascertain that the information you are provided is correct. Realize that what is legal when you begin also may become illegal by the time your child is born. Minimize the risks of that occurring risks by also researching pending legislation in your area regarding surrogacy. (Check with your state's legislative analyst.)

Embryo Ownership

Yet another legal issue involves the "ownership" of the embryos. This typically is not an issue unless the couple whose genes the embryos carry divorce or if the husband or wife dies. For example, if husband and wife both die, who has responsibility for the embryos and how may they be disposed of? For this reason, couples are asked to determine the disposition of any unused embryos, sometimes before they are formed, and certainly afterwards. It is a good idea to provide for this contingency in your will, as well as for an unborn child. It also is important to ensure that, if you relocate, the embryos also can be moved and transferred to a host uterus in your new location. Or, if a spouse dies after the embryos are created and frozen, can the surviving spouse still use the embryos? If that answer is "yes," can a child born from those embryos claim the same benefits as a child who was born before the spouse died? In 1995, the answer was "yes", as the Social Security Administration was directed to award benefits to a child in that situation. Whether an unborn child (or embryo) can inherit remains to be determined.

Some clinics — as well as states — may place some restrictions on the fate of embryos that are not implanted. Some clinics may specify the length of time they will store the embryos. Scientifically, there is as yet no known limit on the length of time a frozen embryo may remain viable so, if your clinic sets limits, discuss such options as paying storage fees or transferring the embryos to another lab when the clinic's specified time expires.

Legal remedies in the case of inadvertent pre-embryo destruction — caused by fire, electrical failure or faulty handling, for example — remain undetermined. Legal remedies for embryo theft are being determined now, based upon Southern California's UCI scandal. In that case, some of the world's top infertility specialists are accused of taking eggs and knowingly implanting them in other women without the consent of the "donors". Whether theft statutes apply, and if they do, whether the charge would be petty theft (for items worth $400 or less) or grand theft (for items worth $400 or more) has yet to be determined. One of the issues will be the value of the eggs themselves. Although the process needed to produce and aspirate those eggs costs a few thousand dollars, an actual monetary figure for the eggs — potential human lives — has not been determined. Attorneys following the case say that a value may never be determined because it is extremely speculative.

Because of that case, California outlawed the intentional transfer of eggs, sperm of embryos without the written consent of the donors and the recipients. Violators may be fined up to $50,000 and imprisoned for up to five years.

International Laws

Australia

Australia currently allows surrogacy but in the event of custody disputes rules in accordance with the best interests of the child. The contract, therefore, is unenforceable and the genetic parents still have to adopt their child as the result of Victorian legislation stating that the woman who gives birth is the legal mother. The law varies among the Australian states.

Canada

By late 1996, Canada was about to ban commercial surrogacy. July 31, 1995, the Royal Commission on New Reproductive Technologies called for a voluntary moratorium on nine practices, including commercial surrogacy arrangements; buying or selling eggs, sperm and embryos; sex selection for non-medical purposes; cloning human embryos; and retrieving eggs from cadavers and fetuses for donation, fertilization or research. The rationale was that those practices threaten human dignity and that women, children and reproduction should not be commodities.

Denmark

In Denmark, legislation was submitted in 1996 to the Danish parliament that would allow the insemination of single women and would allow fertile women to undergo IVF treatments. It also would allow pre-embryos to be diagnosed before they were implanted, and to be stored for three years rather than the one year currently allowed.

France

France banned surrogacy, saying it subverts adoption and violates women's bodies.

Germany

The climate in Germany is not favorable regarding surrogacy, largely because of Green Party influence. Currently, all forms of surrogacy are banned. The law specifically forbids freezing embryos, but defines embryos as fertilized human oocytes after the pronuclei have fused. Therefore, embryos can be frozen one day after insemination, but not after cleavage has occurred.

Great Britain

In Great Britain, commercial surrogacy was banned in the 1985 Surrogacy Arrangements Act, which imposed criminal sanctions upon those engaging in commercial surrogacy. In 1990, non-commercial surrogacy agreements were declared unenforceable in the Human Fertilization and Embryology Act, and were deemed to violate civil law. None-the-less, that same act declares that in the case of a dispute, the genetic parents are the legal parents if:

"(a) the child has been carried by a woman other than the wife as the result of the placing in her of an embryo or sperm and eggs or (by) her artificial insemination;

(b) the gametes of the husband or the wife, or both, were used to bring about the creation of the embryo."

As a result, a child born through surrogacy in Great Britain would be recognized as the child of the commissioning couple upon birth so that adoption would be unnecessary. Additionally, Great Britain's laws mandate that embryos must be disposed of after five years unless the donors consent to freeze them for up to another five years.

Hong Kong

In 1995 and 1996, before Hong Kong returned to the People's Republic of China, recommendations regarding surrogacy called for:

- Banning commercial surrogacy.
- Allowing only genetic IVF and only for infertile, married couples who had no other possible alternative medical treatments.
- Requiring the consent of both the surrogate and her husband.

- Prohibiting women who had never married or born children from becoming surrogates.
- Requiring counseling for the surrogate and for the couple, before, during and after the agreement.

Israel

Israel in 1994 legislated that the genetic parents are the parents of the child and that surrogacy contracts can be enforced. The legislation called for compensating the surrogate for the costs of the pregnancy, delivery, time, suffering and loss of income during the pregnancy. It is important to note that Israel's laws and Jewish laws differ. Israel's laws are a combination of British common law, Ottoman law and Israeli statutory law. In matters governing issues related to marriage and divorce, the Rabbinical Courts of Israel have jurisdiction over Jewish nationals and Jewish residents of Israel, as long as they do not infringe upon basic constitutional freedoms. (See Jewish Law, Chapter 3.)

Japan

In 1993, the Japan Society of Fertility and Sterility published a statement indicating that it does not support surrogacy and had tabled the development of guidelines on that topic. Although surrogacy is not illegal in Japan, neither is it well received. In a 1993 presentation to the Eubios Ethics Institute, Yasuko Shirai indicated that half of all law scholars in Japan disagreed with surrogacy and that 70 percent of a small (46 persons) sample indicated that legislation was needed. Currently the Association of Obstetrics and Gynecology practice self-regulation. A few American clinics have opened offices there (with fees approximately twice those of U.S. surrogacy agreements.)

New Zealand

Openness, information sharing and the dignity of the embryos are the cornerstones of New Zealand's practice of surrogacy. Currently, infertility specialists are prohibited from discriminating (withholding treatment) on the basis of age, marital status, disability or sexual orientation. The Human Rights Act does, however, allow them to withhold treatment if they believe the welfare of any child born to a person would be at risk. That nation furthermore ensures that complete genetic information is available to children born through assisted reproductive techniques and that the donor will in the future be identifiable to the offspring. The basis is both to provide a medical history of the child's biological parents and also as a bow to the Maori tribes, which establish their identity through their lineage. The issue of commercial surrogacy also is tied to the Maori concept of dignity – actually 'mana' in the Maori language. Commercialization shows disrespect for human tissue.

Russia

In Russia, surrogacy is relatively new. As yet, no laws govern maternity, although laws do apply to paternity. Russia's first surrogate program opened February 1996 in St. Petersburg. Called AIST, it recruits surrogates under age 30 for a fee of $10,000, free medical care and $100 in food products. The infertile couple pays the program $25,000. For that, the program is responsible for all legal formalities, recruiting the surrogate and arranging for her payments. There is no contact between the couples and the surrogates, which are chosen based upon photographs and information in a computer database. Foreign couples must send a female relative to Russia to register as the child's legal mother in order for the child to be allowed to leave the country. DNA tests are available if maternity is challenged.

South Africa

By late 1996, South Africa had no legislation governing surrogacy. The Medical Association of South Africa, however, supports surrogacy, "as the final or last option for conceiving a child." That organization recommends that legislation be enacted to avoid the potential for abuse. Specifically, it calls for:

- Compensating the surrogate for actual expenses, including the loss of income, while prohibiting surrogacy for financial gain.

- Allowing surrogacy only for couples with medical reasons that prohibit the woman from becoming pregnant.

- Proper screening of all the parties involved for physical and psychological suitability.

- The creation of an office similar to the Office of the Family Advocate, which would be involved in the screening process and would exercise control and register all surrogacy cases.

- Written and informed consent of all parties involved in the surrogacy process, preferably with legal contracts specifying the agreement.

- At least one genetic link between the commissioning parents and the child.

- Regarding the child as the legitimate child of the commissioning parents.

- Strict confidentiality regarding the identity of the parties, although the children should have the same rights to information regarding their genetic parents as have adopted children.

- Unspecified penalties to discourage illegal surrogacy.

Switzerland

By 1994, Switzerland had no legislation regarding in vitro fertilization or gestational surrogacy. The Canton of Basel, however, attempted to ban IVF even though a referendum in the early 1990s indicated that 74 percent of the Swiss people supported assisted procreation.

5   Choosing a Fertility Clinic

In the U.S. in 1995 there were about 350 infertility clinics — and about 45 in California alone. A list of fertility clinics and their success rates is available from the American Society for Reproductive Medicine. Please note that success rates vary widely depending upon patient age and reason for infertility, as well as with the clinic and the type of technique used.

So far, there is very little oversight of fertility clinics. In 1995, the Centers for Disease Control and Prevention was tasked with developing standard procedures for the laboratories at reproductive centers and with tabulating success rates for infertility clinics, using standard definitions. Implementation, however, is not likely before 1998. The Centers for Disease Control and Prevention in mid-1996 was in the very early stages of developing lab guidelines by surveying other organizations that have voluntary laboratory procedure standards. The accumulation of success rates using standard definitions was at a similar stage. Currently, laboratory accreditation is provided by the College of American Pathologists.

Misconduct among infertility centers is very, very rare — the first and, so far, only case entered the courts in 1995 in California — despite very little oversight regarding who may offer services, types of services and charges. Although there can be no guarantee of perfect laboratory and record-keeping practices, certification by the College of American Pathologists offers one easily verified standard. It is worth asking how the clinic ensures that sperm and, later, fertilized oocytes, are properly labeled and stored to avoid mix-ups. If you opt to freeze any resulting embryos for later possible use, get the numbers of stored embryos in writing promptly. Patients should be told how many oocytes were aspirated, how many were fertilized, how many oocytes were destroyed and how many pre-embryos were cryopreserved. If those numbers change over time, find out why. Don't assume the reason is merely poor record-keeping.

Success Rates

Success rates often are one of the few questions couples ask of a prospective clinic, and they may understandably choose the clinic with the greatest success. However, clinics define success very differently, so be certain you are comparing apples to apples. For example, clinics may consider success as a biochemical pregnancy, in which a blood test showed slightly elevated levels of hCG after about 10 days of implantation. Others consider success a clinical pregnancy, in which an ultrasound shows a fetus with a heartbeat. Also ask about the take-home baby rate for the clinic and for your own situation.

Base rates used to determine the success rate also vary widely, because some clinics count every woman who entered the program, or the number of eggs retrieved, or only the women who produced enough eggs to be retrieved, or only the eggs that became fertilized. As a result, it is possible for a clinic to advertise a success rate of, say 35 percent, without ever having had a live birth.

Even when these differences are accounted for, success rates vary widely. Population data can be controlled so that the statistics are skewed. For example, if clinics only accept those who become pregnant easily, they will have greater success rates than those that accept more difficult cases. The patient population can be skewed by reclassifying patients or their less successful treatment cycles, encouraging patients to cancel treatments when their response is poor or referring patients to other programs. Even good clinics may advise patients to transfer or to cancel unsuccessful treatments, but if the clinic has a habit of that, you may want to continue looking until you find a clinic that has a good track record with patients with your particular diagnoses or age group. Another strategy is to transfer more than four embryos to the uterus at once.

Some fertility clinics also offer egg donor programs, thus providing one more surrogacy option, in which the donor eggs could be implanted into a gestational surrogate. The egg donors themselves probably will be anonymous, but will provide medical and other information — such as intelligence and personality test results, profiles, age, reproductive history, a photo, etc. — to allow a couple to choose a woman as a donor who most closely resembles one of them. According to Shelley Smith, who operates the surrogate and egg donor program at the Huntington Reproductive Center in Pasadena, "If you really like the donor, you don't feel so diminished as a mom." Donors for her program may donate eggs no more than five times.

When interviewing fertility clinics in your area, ask:

- Whether the specialists are board certified endocrinologists and board certified gynecologists.
- Whether the laboratory is accredited by the College of American Pathologists.
- What percentage of potential patients it accepts for treatment.
- What percentage of its treatment cycles are canceled.
- How quickly it begins treatment cycles after the initial consultation.

- The number of embryos transferred at once for someone of your age and condition.
- How it avoids mix-up in the handling and storage of your genetic material.
- Its success rate, what that rate is based upon and what it considers a "success".
- How many IVF procedures it performs annually (The American Fertility Society recommends at least 40).
- The cost of one IVF treatment.
- Whether there is one price for multiple treatments (three cycles for $13,000, for example) or reduced rates for subsequent treatments.
- Whether the lab offers a guarantee or a refund.
- The success rate for women in your age bracket, undergoing IVF specifically.
- The success rate for your specific condition.
- How many IVF procedures at that clinic result in "take home" babies.
- Number of years in practice treating infertility.
- Experience with IVF.
- Number of embryos implanted in one woman at once.
- Exactly what the process will involve.
- How the clinic would inform you and your surrogate of developments.
- Whether it has the capability to cryopreserve any extra embryos.
- How will the clinic ascertain that the stored embryos are yours.

- Who will store the embryos.
- How long may they be stored.
- With which hospitals they are associated.
- Whether you will be seen primarily by one physician or several physicians in the practice.
- That both the couple and the surrogate will have direct access to information regarding the procedures, their success or failure and any resulting pregnancy. (Neither party should have to receive this information second-hand.)
- The overall "take-home" baby rate.
- The pregnancy rate for couples *in your specific situation* working with surrogates.
- The take-home baby rate for your specific situation.
- Cost of procedures for you and the surrogate.
- The specific treatments for you and the surrogate.
- How long the clinic has operated.
- How long it has performed IVF procedures.
- The background of the fertility specialists practicing there.
- Whether the clinic has been involved in any lawsuits and their outcome.
- Their policy regarding egg retrieval and embryo storage.
- Whether the husband may be present during the oocyte retrieval.
- How they can ensure that your embryos will be properly counted and labeled.
- Their take-home baby rate using frozen embryos.

- Costs for multiple IVF cycles.
- Whether a discount is offered if the treatments are unsuccessful.
- Whether the clinic operates a surrogate program itself or has a working relationship with a program.
- Whether the clinic and its lab are open weekends for procedures.
- Their hours and your access to personnel if you have questions or concerns.
- How patients are educated about the procedures and the reasons they are used.
- Whether the clinic has a cost reduction program.
- Costs for the surrogate.
- Whether they use fax and/or email to exchange information that may be needed quickly.

Additionally, the Genetics & IVF Institute (Fairfax, VA) recommends finding a clinic with extensive experience, looking in a broad geographic area, asking physicians where they themselves would go for infertility treatment, and contacting former patients if possible. Additionally, read the medical literature to identify the innovators in infertility treatments. This can be done by accessing computer databases like Medline (a medical research database) or IQuest (reference databases) and performing a search. These services and similar services are available through online services like CompuServe or America OnLine, via direct access using an Internet account, and through some universities and public libraries.

Because there is relatively little oversight of fertility clinics, take pains to choose a reputable clinic with a high rate of "take-home" babies for couples in your medical situation. A list of infertility clinics, along with medical, legal and psychological resources is available to members of the Organization of Parents Through Surrogacy. Lists of infertility clinics also are available from Resolve and the American Society for Reproductive Medicine (see Appendix B for contact information), and from your gynecologist. In all likelihood, you already have chosen a fertility clinic for previous diagnosis and treatment. Regardless of your experience, it may be worthwhile to explore their views and experience with surrogacy.

Costs

The cost of IVF cycle varies widely depending upon the clinic, and is not necessarily related to success rates. In 1993 in the U.S., average cost for one IVF cycle was $6,233. Three years later, one IVF cycle may cost between $4,500 to $15,000, and insurance companies tend to not offer full coverage for infertility treatments. In fact, according to Diane Batzofin at the Huntington Reproductive Center, 85 percent of its IVF patients are not covered for the treatments. Massachusetts has mandated that insurers reimburse their clients for all IVF treatments, and six other states have also mandated some form of reimbursement. (Appendix D.)

Costs for single or twin pregnancies using IVF, without surrogacy, were calculated at an average of $39,000 in the U.S. Because repeated cycles of IVF can be so expensive, some fertility clinics are offering performance-based discount plans for multiple cycles, and some even offer a partial refund if no pregnancy results. At Huntington Reproductive Center in Pasadena and Encino, California, for example, the cost for one IVF cycle in Spring 1996 was $4,500 and the cost for two IVF cycles ranged from $6,700 to $7,500, depending upon the age of the patient. Its refund program "...refunds 90 percent of medical fees paid by qualifying couples if they fail to achieve a pregnancy beyond the first trimester after the transfer of all the embryos (fresh and frozen) that are obtained from a single egg retrieval. The costs associated with the treatment are increased according to the age of the women." That package included the costs for ultrasound monitoring, RIA lab tests, egg retrieval, IVF lab, embryo transfer, post-transfer blood tests, pregnancy related blood tests and ultrasounds and frozen embryo transfers. Microhatching and microfertilization were refunded at 50 percent at the Huntington Reproductive Center.

The American Medical Association opposes performance-based fees for any medical service or specialty. The AMA's Opinions on Confidentiality, Advertising and Communications Media Relations, states:

"Because physicians have an ethical obligation to share medical advances, it is unlikely that a physician will have a truly exclusive or unique skill or remedy. Claims that imply such a skill or remedy therefore can be deceptive. Statements that a physician (excels in a procedure) in a particular geographic area, if true, however, are permissible. Similarly, a statement that a physician has cured or successfully treated a large number of cases involving a particular serious ailment is deceptive if it implies a certainty of result and creates unjustified and misleading expectations in prospective patients."

Choosing a Physician

Beyond choosing a reputable clinic, you also must select a qualified physician. Choose someone who is board certified in both reproductive endocrinology and gynecology and who has practiced in this field successfully for some time. If the problem is male infertility, you also may be referred to a urologist who specializes in infertility or to an andrologist — a urological sub-specialist who studies the diseases of males and particularly of the male reproductive tract. Board certification is particularly important because any gynecologist can claim to be a fertility specialist. Board certification ensures that the physician has passed national examinations on that specialty.

Get as much information about these physicians as you can, including length of time at this clinic, time in practice, where they graduated medical school, where they completed their internship and residency, where and whether they have completed fellowships in areas related to infertility and whether they are comfortable working with surrogate situations. You can research physicians by phoning the physician referral desk at one of the leading hospitals in your area to ask about their infertility specialists, phoning the fertility clinic in question, looking in the Directory of Medical Specialists, phoning the American College of Endocrinology for a list of physicians in your area or checking their directory, or obtaining a geographic list of specialists from RESOLVE, a support group for infertile couples, and then phoning its national headquarters for specific physicians' biographies.

Once you have chosen a clinic and a physician, you are ready for the first consultation. The physician will review your medical histories, so have your files sent to the clinic from your gynecologist, family physician or previous infertility specialist. Expect to have a sperm analysis conducted and an evaluation of your reproductive system. A treatment plan will be identified. Take notes during the consultation. A lot of information typically is provided, including medical and financial details, and patients easily can become overwhelmed.

Additionally, talk with your specialist to determine whether your treatment is considered experimental, innovative or standard. Experimental treatments are still evolving as research is conducted. It is often too early to predict results from such treatments. Innovative treatments have passed the experimental stage but are not yet mainstream practices. They are likely to have good results in the cases in which they have been used. Standard treatments have an obvious track record but may not be the most effective option for your situation. Whichever phase of development your treatment is in, ask how long it has been used and its results in situations like yours. The use of an experimental or innovative treatment is not a reason to avoid a clinic, but the risks and potential benefits should be explained thoroughly so you are fully informed. Also, you should know why your physician prefers an experimental or innovative treatment for your case and how its results are likely to compare to those of the standard treatment. Be aware that experimental treatments will not be covered by insurance. Carriers are willing only to pay for approved treatments, in an effort to make the most effective use of their money for the largest number of clients. So, if an experimental treatment is used, ask whether the clinic offers any price reductions for that treatment.

If you are unhappy with your treatment, get a second opinion or change physicians or clinics. It may be time to change if:

- You need to remind the physician or staff that certain tests have already been conducted.
- The treatment plan seems haphazard.
- The same treatment plan is continued unsuccessfully for three or four cycles.
- Communications are poor and questions are dismissed

without the level of detail you need.
- Therapies are not monitored closely.

Remember that a poor bedside manner is not indicative of a poorly qualified doctor. Some infertility specialists are brilliant in the laboratory but have poor interpersonal skills. Some are so focused upon their work they may forget to say "hello" to their patients!

Making Time for Appointments

It may sound silly, but be certain to arrange your business schedule around the infertility specialist's needs. Most clinics will be open early in the morning and on weekends, so appointments at 7:30 a.m. are usual and can help minimize time away from work. If you must travel great distances for appointments, talk with the clinic in advance to try to arrange the most suitable appointment times.

6 Demographics of Surrogates and Surrogate Couples

Throw away any stereotypes you have about surrogates and the infertile couples who have babies thanks to surrogates and IVF. The people can't be pigeonholed.

The couples who choose to enter into surrogacy arrangements in the hopes of having a baby are infertile. Surrogacy is a last resort for couples who accept their infertility. It is not an option for people who aren't willing to lose their figures to pregnancy or take time from busy careers. The vast majority of surrogates, agencies and clinics won't work with people in those circumstances, and some states and nations require that a couple be infertile before permitting them to engage in surrogacy.

Most — but not all — couples who opt for surrogacy have undergone numerous fertility treatments and spent tens of thousands of dollars in this quest. This doesn't mean they are wealthy, however. It's not unusual for couples to refinance their homes or take second mortgages to finance the endeavor. Their ages range from the late 20s to early 50s, although most are over age 35, and tend to be from the middle or upper classes. They often are successful professionals. Surrogacy is their last option in their efforts to have a child who is genetically theirs. They try to find the best clinic, the best doctor, the best surrogate, the best method and the highest success rate. No studies have been conducted to determine the demographics of couples who choose surrogacy.

In 1982 — the most recent period for which data is available — the National Center for Health Statistics reported that 2.4 million married couples — about 8.5 percent of the population — were infertile. For that study, "infertile" was defined as having 12 months or more of unprotected intercourse without pregnancy resulting. Infertility rates for women between ages 30 and 34 was 14 percent and for women between ages 35 and 39 was 25 percent. Additionally, "Black and poor women have higher rates of infertility than white and middle class women, largely because of poorer nutrition and health care," according to John Robertson in his book, Children of Choice. About one million couples use an infertility clinic each year.

Not every couple who wants to have a child through surrogacy is accepted. Medical or psychological unsuitability are the primary reasons, but some surrogacy agencies — and, for that matter, some fertility specialists — will refuse for other reasons, including the age of the parents. For example, once a woman has undergone menopause, many in this field are uncomfortable initiating a pregnancy although some women in that situation have become mothers. The Catholic Church in 1995 issued a decision discouraging post-menopausal women from becoming mothers using assisted reproductive technologies, and some nations also discourage the practice.

Katie Brophy of Surrogate Family Services in Louisville, KY, said, "There are some very obvious reasons a couple would be turned away, such as mental illness, and the couple must be able to financially afford the program even if 'the worst' should happen." Marital status is another potential reason to be turned away by a surrogacy program. Married couples are preferred over single individuals by some agencies. The reasoning, according to Cristie Montgomery at Surrogate Parenting Services (Laguna Niguel, CA), is that, "Most surrogates have an ideal image of the family they are helping and are not comfortable working with a single person."

The "average" surrogate is even more difficult to profile. Surrogates come from all walks of life, with all levels of education. The one thing they have in common is a desire to give another couple the joy of parenthood. They tend to love children and generally consider motherhood their most fulfilling role. Typically, they have easy pregnancies and enjoy being pregnant.

The perceived stereotype says these women are prompted by money and so, therefore, are vulnerable to exploitation, and that surrendering the infant to its genetic parents is traumatic, according to Dr. Betsey P. Aigen, in a three-year study of 200 potential surrogates applying to the Surrogate Mother Program of New York (now called the Childbirth Consultation Service). "There is little actual data to substantiate these claims," she concluded in her preliminary study.

At the Infertility Center of New York, now called the Infertility Center of America and relocated to Indianapolis, Indiana, surrogates are between the ages of 18 and 35 and are from a wide variety of races and ethnic backgrounds and may be married or single. That particular program does not require surrogates to have children of their own, but many other program do. Other surrogacy program coordinators say their surrogates typically have at least a high school education, and some also include professionals as surrogates. Women who become surrogates at Surrogate Parenting Services typically also are married with an average of two young children, and "They love being mothers," Montgomery added. Not all surrogates have completed their families, however. Some want another child, but not necessarily now, but enjoy being pregnant and so are willing to help another couple build a family.

In Aigen's study, the mean age of the entire group was 26. Half were married. More than 70 percent were mothers and 16 percent had some connection to adoption, either through personal experience or that or friends or relatives. Some 40 percent had undergone at least one abortion. The group was predominately white and Christian with an average educational level of 13.3 years. More than 70 percent were employed full- or part-time with an average annual income of more than $24,000. One fourth of these women had household incomes of more than $35,000 per year. On average, they had been interested in becoming a surrogate for 1.5 years, Aigen reported and some 70 percent wanted to meet the couple. She concluded that most of these women are parents who knew what the experience of carrying and bearing a child is about. "They are not naïve, passive dupes who are desperate and susceptible to exploitation," she wrote.

Only a few studies have been conducted to determine what type of woman becomes a surrogate, and those study results rarely differed. One of the earliest, conducted by Hiliary Hanafin in 1984, now a psychologist at the Center for Surrogate Parenting, found that about 65 percent of the surrogates she studied were conservative or traditional women who held conventional beliefs about a woman's role in the family and who had never done anything unusual in their lives. The other third were nontraditional or independent and had chosen to become single mothers or had participated in nontraditional activities like racing sailboats or joining the military. A more recent survey, conducted by Helena Ragone, found that fewer than five percent of the surrogates she interviewed were nontraditional using Hanafin's definition.

Agencies list the reasons for wanting to become surrogates as a genuine desire to help someone else have a family, having infertile relatives or friends, being adopted themselves, financial concerns, the need to be the center of attention and even the search for the perfect birth experience without the desire for another baby of their own. Many of these women had dreamed of being a surrogate before they learned the technology was available to make it possible. Money, of course, is one motivator — surrogates have used the money to help with a down payment on a home, to relocate for better jobs, stay home with their children rather than putting them in daycare, pay off large debts and many other reasons — but money should never be the sole reason for becoming a surrogate. If the reimbursement for her expenses — including a partial housing, clothing and food allowance — was treated as an hourly wage, it would only be a few dollars an hour and, therefore, lower than the U.S. minimum wage. For some surrogates, there also may be a social enticement. They like the attention they receive when pregnant, and also enjoy the extra attention of being a surrogate. That role catapults them into a new social setting, meeting professionals and other surrogates while reaffirming their commitment to family and giving what is often called "the ultimate gift" to an infertile couple. Surrogacy is not something that just anyone can do, and surrogates derive special pleasure from that knowledge.

Those accepted as surrogates in Aigen's study were individuals for whom surrogacy would be a positive emotional experience, who had a high tolerance of frustration, a history of enjoyable pregnancies, good relationships with their own children and a supportive home environment.

About 40 percent of the women who participated in Aigen's study were rejected as potential surrogates by the Surrogate Mother Program of New York. Potential surrogates were rejected because of ambivalence about becoming surrogates, conflicts regarding the responsibility or the energy and resources required, an overwhelming desire for the fee involved, the possibility of not surrendering the baby or of experiencing emotional pain because of the need to surrender the child, a life crisis, family crisie, an identity crisis, a desire to use surrogacy to remediate a previous trauma, a poor emotional condition or dishonesty.

Those reasons for rejecting a surrogate will hold true for most agencies. Beyond those concerns, past arrests or deviant behavior also should disqualify a candidate. Some agencies also like to ensure that the surrogate is in control of her own life, and that she is responsible and can follow directions. Some agencies also are concerned about her support system of friends and family during the pregnancy. A woman who has experienced a miscarriage or an abortion may be considered if those events were several years ago and if she has one of her own children living with her now.

Before a woman becomes a surrogate, she should undergo rigorous psychological screening by a licensed psychologist to identify any personality characteristics that would hinder her ability to fulfill a surrogacy contract. When investigating surrogate agencies, ask if they have an established relationship with a psychologist and how that person screens potential surrogates. Once a woman is accepted as a potential surrogate by a surrogate program, those programs tend to take special pains to help ensure that she really feels that the child she will carry, or is carrying, belongs to her couple. Methods include encouraging her to bond with the couple rather than the child, emphasizing her responsibilities to the couple, emphasizing her own sense of honor and requiring her to attend meetings of a surrogate support group.

In the vast majority of cases, surrogates do not regard the children they carry for other couples as their own. Surrogates do not want more children of their own right now and have gone through a great deal of time and trouble to conceive a child for another couple. In the case of gestational surrogates, there are no genetic links between surrogate and child, further distancing the two. Surrogates often say that their pregnancies as surrogates "felt" different than when they carried their own children. The intense emotional involvement they had with their own children during their prenatal development was lacking during pregnancy as a surrogate.

The profile of surrogates has remained relatively stable over the years, although the development of IVF procedures (using the prospective father's sperm and his wife's eggs) brought more potential surrogates into the programs, according to several surrogacy program coordinators. Another change from the early days of surrogacy is that today it's not unusual for surrogates to want to be a surrogate more than once. In fact, Ragone's study found that about 30 percent of surrogates were interested in repeating the experience. Some may want to do this again only for their original couple, but many others have changed both couples and programs.

The Children

Children born through IVF and surrogacy are some of the most wanted, planned-for children on earth. Worldwide, since 1978, more than 30,000 children have been born thanks to IVF. More than 8,230 have been born in the U.S. between 1990 and 1994. Their parents have gone through an inordinate amount of effort, pain, frustration and, yes, expense, just to bring them into the world. They tend to be born to older parents — those in their 30s and 40s. Now, although older parents are becoming more common, they are still in the minority. Of the 3.8 million babies born in the U.S. in 1987, only 250,000 were born to mothers between the ages of 35 and 39. And that fact alone makes a difference in the world that children born thanks to surrogacy will experience.

There are some definite disadvantages to having children late in life, for the parents as well as for the children. For example, most people simply don't have the energy at 45 that they had at 25. That means that sleepless nights with a sick child are harder for you and that your child is less likely to remember you rolling on the floor playing, getting involved in a game of softball or even going outside to play catch.

A frequent complaint of the children of older parents is that they grew up too soon, often because they spent most of their childhood around adults. They spent more time reading or drawing alone than playing with other children. The benefit, of course, is that as young adults they relate quite well to other adults and show a marked maturity that can emerge as a competitive edge as they enter the workplace. They also are more likely to be their parents only children or, if not, to have brothers and sisters who are significantly older and already may have left home. Another frequent complaint is that children of older parents tend to be lonely. Part of the reason is that families begun later in life tend to be smaller and that the children's cousins may be old enough to be their parents. At this stage, their grandparents often are rather old themselves and aren't really able to participate as fully in their grandchildren's lives as are younger grandparents.

As young adults, children born to older parents may be thrust into the role of caretaker early. Health statistics show that people are most likely to develop a disabling disease at age 75. If you had a child at age 42, your child will be 33 then. That means that while your child is establishing a career and family, he or she may also have to shoulder the burden of looking after parents who are ill or who need assisted living arrangements. With modern mobility, this means frequent and disruptive trips home – often cross-country — for adults who may not have acquired enough life experience yet to deal effectively with chronically- or terminally-ill or disabled parents.

All of those complaints can be tempered by parents who love their children and devote time to them, ensuring that even if the parents aren't as physically active as the child might wish, they have friends and outlets for that energy. These children also will have parents who, presumably, have matured sufficiently to happily forego many of their accustomed pleasures in order to be with their children. Additionally, these children are more likely to have financial advantages their friends may lack, such as a savings plan for college or more expendable family income.

Remember, as parents, that there also are certain benefits to having children later in life. First, you've have the opportunity to experience more of life and so are less likely to resent the pursuits you give up because of your children. Also, older parents tend to be more stable than younger ones — incomes are higher, the parents have been married longer and are less likely to divorce. A 1982 study found that children born to older mothers tended to have higher IQs than those born to younger mothers but, beyond that, children born to older parents tend to have better-educated parents who in turn talk more to their babies, are somewhat more patient and tend to buy them more interesting toys to play with. They also are more likely to use praise than criticism to teach their children.

With all that said, a study conducted by Susan Golombok at City University in London and published in the April 1995 issue of Child Development indicates that the quality of parenting in families with a child conceived using in vitro fertilization or donor insemination exceeds that in well-functioning families in which the child was conceived naturally. "The findings suggest that genetic ties are less important for family functioning than a strong desire for parenthood," the researchers reported, although both cases had genetic ties to at least one parent.

What to Tell Your Child

During the surrogate selection process you may be asked what you will tell your children about the surrogate, with the obvious implication that you will tell them about the surrogate's involvement. What you tell them and when you tell them is up to you, but telling them is strongly recommended. Secrets do tend to come out, and usually at the worst times. It doesn't have to be a big announcement. Experiences tend to be passed from one generation to the next in the form of stories. That's probably how you learned about your own birth, and it's a good way to tell them about their own. The explanation that, "I couldn't carry you in my tummy like other mommies, so another lady carried you for me," will suffice for years, until they ask for more details. Once they're adults and are planning families of their own, they may want the specific medical details – including the medications taken, the type of fertilization process required and the exact causes of your infertility – because it may affect their own ability to procreate. If you keep a diary that includes dates of medical appointments, drugs prescribed and the reasons you were infertile and sought the help of a surrogate, providing the information your adult children need will be easy. Remember to include your thoughts and feelings during the process, too, and the developmental milestones as the embryo developed into a child. (Or place a copy of this book in your files, along with the details of your own experiences.)

7 Finding and Choosing a Surrogate and a Surrogate Program

Deciding to work through a reputable program is a good first step towards entering into a surrogacy agreement. The simple reason is that this streamlines the process by eliminating much of the guesswork and legwork, helps ensure that the parents-to-be and the surrogate are a good match and provides an invaluable and objective go-between who can help keep the relationship smooth between the surrogate and the parents. A good program represents a safe haven for both parties to express their fears and concerns about the process and about each other and, importantly, reach some resolution. Surrogate program coordinators play a large role in helping set the tone of the working relationship between the surrogate and her couple. For example, they subtly — and sometimes not-so-subtly — reinforce the concept that the surrogate is carrying another couple's child by referring to the couple as the mom and the dad, as well as by their names. They also may tell the surrogate a bit of the couple's history of infertility, to help her understand some of the emotional turmoil they have gone through and to develop some empathy for them.

Why Use a Surrogacy Program?

Although many states ban intermediaries such as surrogate agencies, the American Academy of Pediatrics (AAP) encourages their use. In a July 1992 policy statement, the AAP recommended that the surrogate parenting agreement be approved by an agency that can provide social work, legal and psychological services to ensure that the interests of all involved parties are adequately protected. That includes surrogacy programs and adoption agencies.

Program directors say that working with a surrogacy program gives couples a broad range of candidates, the benefit of experience and expertise and a guide through the necessary legal procedures. Screening and support are two other very important aspects. According to Cristie Montgomery of Surrogate Parenting Services, "Working with a program minimizes room for misunderstandings, and a psychologist is in regular contact," to minimize the other problems. It also helps ensure confidentiality and allows all the parties to review their options. Expect a program also to have lists of specialists for medical, legal and psychological services who are familiar with surrogacy. "There are all kinds of possible problems other than changing one's mind," Montgomery said.

A surrogate program, depending upon local law, may be responsible for finding a pool of surrogates and couples. The program also should ensure that both parties are screened medically and — for the surrogate and sometimes for the couple — psychologically. The program also should ensure that the surrogate and the couple are, in fact, who and what they say they are. Does the program accept information at face value or does it verify that information, for example, checking credit reports, school transcripts, birth certificates of any children or checking for criminal records or cases or child abuse?

The program obtains a detailed personal profile of each of the parties and provides that information to potential matches, allowing them to decide, based upon that information, whether to meet and discuss forming a surrogacy team. If the couple and the surrogate decides to work together, the program coordinator ensures that the potential parents, the surrogate and her spouse or partner undergo medical testing to ensure that all are free of communicable diseases, including AIDS.

The program coordinator also should ensure that you each sign a contract specifying the details of the surrogacy agreement, expense reimbursement and reimbursement schedules and how legal issues at birth will be handled. The contract also may include a confidentiality clause to protect the identities of the surrogate as well as the prospective parents (so avoiding unwanted publicity) and may specify that the surrogate and couple cease contact after the child's birth. Additionally, the program coordinator should ensure that the couple provides for the unborn child in their wills and that an escrow account is established to pay the surrogate's expenses during the pregnancy.

Typically, the program coordinator checks with the surrogate and the prospective parents every few weeks, usually after a medical appointment, for updates on the progress, to answer questions and to help ensure that the relationship remains untroubled. If the surrogate and prospective parents are separated geographically (some U.S. agencies have worked with U.S.-based surrogates and international parents -to-be), the program coordinator also will forward progress updates to the prospective parents and provide a little extra encouragement to the surrogate. The program coordinator may come to the first appointment with the fertility specialist, to the implantation itself and to other important examinations.

The program coordinator also should ensure that the surrogate attends regular counseling sessions — ideally with a group of other surrogates. Many have informal gatherings of the prospective parents, as well, to exchange ideas and encouragement. Before the baby is born, California-based program coordinators also will ensure that a court order gives custody of the child to the couple. Program coordinators in other areas should ensure that all of the paperwork is in order to minimize any confusion as to the identity of the child's legal parents and to streamline the legal process, according to the laws in their state or nation. The program coordinator also may be present at the birth. The details of a program coordinator's involvement should be spelled out in the service agreement.

Surrogacy agencies come in all sizes, from home-based businesses staffed entirely by a single program coordinator to large centers with several staff members. Both types can provide the services you need. The smaller program may be more personal and the larger firm more efficient, but that really depends upon the program itself. As one example, at the Infertility Center of America, home phone numbers of program personnel are given to the couple and surrogate at the seventh month of pregnancy, to provide whatever services are needed, 24-hours per day. With a home-based business, that number may be available from the beginning — but not necessarily. Likewise, the larger program may have a larger pool of professionals — attorneys, obstetricians, psychologists, etc. — who are familiar with surrogacy and upon whom you can rely. A small program, particular a relatively new one, may have only one or two professionals who are sufficiently familiar with surrogacy to provide sound advice. Some agencies also have newsletters and even provide parenting information after the baby is born.

I strongly recommend using a program coordinator, even — or perhaps especially — if the surrogate and prospective parents are close friends or family. This is an emotionally charged time for everyone involved, and misunderstandings can occur easily. The presence of someone who is intimately familiar with the process can help you avoid emotional and legal pitfalls.

Depending upon where you live, finding a surrogacy program coordinator may be difficult. Major metropolitan areas, naturally, are more likely to have a few agencies to choose from than are smaller cities. But even the Los Angeles area has only a handful. The best place to begin the search is with your gynecologist or fertility specialist. The fertility specialist, in particular, should be able to recommend at least one program for you to interview. Beyond this, some surrogacy agencies advertise in parenting magazines and in the classified advertisements of major newspapers. Two national organizations, the Organization of Parents Through Surrogacy (OPTS) and RESOLVE, also may be able to provide the names of surrogacy agencies in your area. (Appendix C.)

Screening Agencies

After you've located some agencies, interview them. You can do this over the phone or in person. Questions to ask include:

- Why did you form a surrogacy program?
- Do you recruit your own surrogates? How?
- How do you know your surrogates and couples are who and what they proclaim themselves to be?
- Will you work with a surrogate recruited by the couple?
- Do you coordinate logistics among the couple, surrogate, physicians, clinic, support groups, and any other entities involved in this procedure?
- Is there are fee for an initial consultation or for informational meetings and interviews?

A Matter of Trust

- What are your fees?
- Under what circumstances are the fees, or any portion thereof, refundable?
- What are your surrogates' fees?
- What other expenses will you incur on behalf of the surrogate?
- When are these fees incurred?
- Are there additional fees if multiples are carried or born?
- In the case of multiples, when are those payments made?
- How is reimbursement arranged?
- If the parents choose to have another child through surrogacy, does the program discount its fees?
- What other fees are involved in the surrogacy process?
- Has your program ever been involved in a lawsuit? If so, why? What was the outcome?
- How do you deal with contested surrogacy situations?
- Has a surrogate in your program ever changed her mind and tried to keep a baby?
- May I talk with some of the people who have worked with you in the past?
- How many couples do you work with at any one time?
- Do you encourage contact between the surrogate and the couple prior to the birth? To what extent?
- Is there a waiting list?
- How long would it take to get started?

The Guide to Gestational Surrogacy

- How long have you been a surrogacy program coordinator?
- How old is this program?
- How many couples have you worked with?
- How many babies have been born through your program?
- How do you prepare for potentially premature births?
- What are the financial obligations of the couple in the event of a miscarriage, abortion or stillbirth?
- How do you select and screen your surrogates?
- Have any of the surrogates worked with you again?
- How do you select and screen your potential parents?
- Have any worked with you again?
- Who would you refuse to work with?
- What happens if we find our own surrogate? Will the costs be different?
- What services do you provide for the surrogate?
- Which services do you insist upon and which services are optional?
- Will you complete the legal work that is necessary after the baby is born?
- If you have an attorney you work with, are we obligated to work with him or her or may we work with another?
- What happens if a surrogate or couple drops out of the program once a match is made?
- How long will you work with us in the case of failed pregnancies?

A Matter of Trust

- What services do you provide for the potential parents?
- Do you provide psychological counseling for the surrogates? For the parents?
- What type of surrogate/couple interaction do you encourage during the process?
- What information do you provide about potential matches prior to meeting?
- Where do the meetings generally occur?
- If you have informal gatherings for your couples or surrogates, may we attend one?
- Do you require couples to attend your gatherings?
- May we see a copy of your contracts?
- May our attorney review your contracts?
- What happens after we sign your contract?
- Do you maintain contact with the couple or surrogate after the birth?
- Do you maintain a medical registry to track the health of the surrogate or the baby after its birth?
- Have you personally gone through the process as a surrogate, couple or egg donor?
- Are gifts usually given for special occasions?
- How do you keep abreast of current legislation regarding surrogacy and respond to them?
- Do the couples and surrogates meet in your program or are all parties anonymous?
- Do you have a list of health care insurers that accept surrogacy situations?

Open vs. Closed Programs

Not all surrogacy agencies are alike. They can be divided into "open" and "closed" programs. The open programs do the best job of balancing the needs of the surrogate with those of the couple. Typically, the open programs believe that positive information about surrogacy can counteract much of the bad publicity it has received. Open programs encourage the surrogate and the couple to interact, thus helping the surrogate to bond with the couple rather than with the child. The surrogate and the couple exchange phone numbers and addresses and may get together for dinner or lunch or other outings. Letters and phone calls are direct, without program involvement. In these programs there is great emphasis upon consideration of each other's feelings. Surrogates in these programs are more likely to have a positive experience, according to research conducted by University of Massachusetts - Boston anthropologist Helena Ragone.

Closed programs generally forbid interaction between the couple and the surrogate and all communications between the two are relayed through the program. Surrogates may be chosen from a photo and a brief biographical sketch. The program may hold the belief that surrogates are self-selecting and therefore may have inadequate screening as well as inadequate emotional support for its surrogates. Couples in these programs have little responsibility for the surrogate, other than financial.

Other than these differences, the rest are relatively minor. Some surrogacy agencies are operated by lawyers well-versed in the legal aspects of surrogacy and, often, adoptions. Others are operated by former surrogates, infertility nurses, physicians or others interested in surrogacy. Some chose the business as a good business opportunity that matched their professional training. Others chose this because they truly love bringing the joy of a new life to people otherwise unable to have children to whom they are genetically linked. The reasons are as varied as the people themselves. Also, some agencies cater more to the surrogates and some more to the couple. Some strike a good balance and serve both well. There's no one "best" type of program or reason for founding a program . Each one offers tradeoffs in areas of expertise and personal involvement. Choose the program coordinator with whom you are most comfortable.

Remember that surrogacy agencies are unregulated in the U.S. Virtually anyone can declare themselves to be a surrogacy program, regardless of experience in that field. Before you sign a contract, check out the program carefully and talk with former clients, if at all possible.

The Personality Profile

As couples and surrogates sign up with a program, they complete a personality profile that is used as the basis for the eventual match. This is a fairly detailed document. Be prepared to discuss hobbies, life goals, philosophy of life, why you want to work with a surrogate, family medical history, happiest and saddest childhood memories, best and worst subjects in school, extracurricular activities, family expectations, religious background, relationship with parents, what you expect from the surrogate during the process and your opinions on abortion, selective reduction and amniocentesis. Details of the questionnaire will vary, depending upon the program you choose. Some focus primarily on the most pertinent details relating to surrogacy. Others delve into life's minutia and include a range of questions that have no bearing upon success as a surrogate couple but that help paint a picture of you currently and during the formative periods of life.

Sample Personality Inventory:

- Name.
- Address and phone number.
- Occupation and employer.
- Criminal record.
- Any previous involvement with reproductive medicine.
- Height.
- Weight.
- Date married.
- Previous marriages.
- Weight change within the past five years, and reason.
- Ethnic origin.
- Special interests.
- Goals.
- Major achievements.
- Philosophy of life.
- The importance of money in your life.
- Childhood personality.
- Academic record.
- Extracurricular activities when in school.
- Worst academic subjects.
- College, major, degree(s).
- Religious affiliation and its importance.
- Experiences abroad.

- One's relationship with one's parents.
- How you were disciplined as a child.
- Experience with physical, sexual or psychological abuse.
- Important qualities for your surrogate to have.
- Expectations for that relationship during pregnancy and after the birth?
- If the child wishes to meet the surrogate someday, how would you feel?
- Would you like to attend the medical appointments with the surrogate?
- If the child has severe physical or mental abnormalities, would you want to terminate the pregnancy?
- How do you feel about selective reduction?

Choosing a Surrogate

Sometimes a program will have a pool of surrogates ready, just waiting for the "perfect" match. More often, the number of couples awaiting surrogates is greater than the number of available surrogates. As a result, you may have to wait a few weeks or a few months before a match would even be possible. Bear in mind that programs that do not have a waiting list may not screen potential surrogates as carefully as you would like.

You may be tempted to allow a friend or relative to be your surrogate. Be careful. You will have all of the usual difficulties, plus the complications of social contact. For example, how will you feel after the child is born and your surrogate is around the child often? Will your surrogate feel she has a special claim on the child or upon your friendship? How will you feel if your relationship dissolves or if you have disagreements regarding prenatal care? If you choose this route you still should go through all of the steps that you would if you chose a surrogate who was unknown to you, even if the surrogate is your own mother, to protect her, your relationship and your own families.

Typically, prospective parents will be told about several potential surrogates, in broad terms initially. For example, first names and such general information as city of residence, marital status, age, race, weight, height, occupation, whether she has health insurance and her reason for wanting to be a surrogate may be presented initially. Screen these brief profiles carefully.

Do you prefer someone who lives in the same city as you and who can stop by easily, or would you rather minimize the potential for contact and choose a surrogate who must travel an hour or more to visit? Your answer affects where your baby will be born and your ability to attend medical appointments. Your involvement in the pregnancy also affects your surrogate's ability to consider this baby as yours. This is a personal decision, but also may be governed by the laws where you live. Because some nations have banned surrogacy, some couples actually fly to the U.S. to find a surrogate and a surrogate program, and correspond regularly through the program and electronically. Such situations can work just as well as those in which the couple and the surrogate are geographically close.

Marital status may be of minor importance, but the presence of a husband, even if he is out of the country during the pregnancy, can provide comfort and moral support and, if he is with his wife the first few months of the process, can be invaluable in helping her through the regimen of injections that are necessary to synchronize her menstrual cycle with that of the prospective mother. It's also quite nice if he is active in his own children's lives, thus relieving her of some of the pressures single mothers face. If the surrogate is single, it may be worthwhile to explore her reasons for that and, perhaps, her ability to commit. Additionally, determine whether she has a reliable support network of family or friends nearby.

Is she mature and of a background that at least indicates compatible social norms? Age may be a consideration. Is she too young or too old to withstand the physical and psychological rigors of pregnancy and delivery? Although most surrogates are between the ages of 18 and 34, a 51 year old mother acted as a surrogate for her daughter in London in 1996, making her one of only about six women in the world to have become surrogate mothers for their grandchildren. If she is of another race, will that bother any of you? Will you feel that society will assume you are exploiting her? Will it concern you to tell your child that the woman who carried him or her was of another race?

Her occupation may affect the pregnancy or her ability to function well throughout it. Is she in a safe environment or is she exposed to violent behavior or toxic chemicals? Is her job physically active? Can she perform her job easily throughout the pregnancy? Does she plan to continue to work throughout the pregnancy or will she use this time to be with her own children? If bedrest is prescribed during the pregnancy can she still care for her family both financially and physically?

Whether she has health insurance may alter your costs for the pregnancy. If she is insured, her carrier may cover the prenatal care and delivery. If she is uninsured, she may not be able to become insured easily and a policy that would accept her may require a waiting period of several months before it will reimburse any pregnancy-related expenses. The obvious preference is to work with a woman who already has maternity coverage, because insurance for surrogates is becoming increasingly difficult to obtain.

It may seem churlish to discriminate against a woman because of her weight but obese women are twice as likely to have children with neural tube defects than are women who are not significantly overweight, according to a report by Gary M. Shaw, DPH, the March of Dimes Birth Defects Foundation, in the April 9, 1995 Journal of the American Medical Association (JAMA). Nutritional factors, such as zinc or folic acid intake, did not protect the children born of obese women, the study reported. A separate study conducted by Martha M. Werler, Sc.D. from Boston University's School of Public Health also indicated that the risk of neural tube defects increased with greater pre-pregnancy weight and was not linked to folic acid intake, which in women of normal weights protects their fetuses from neural tube defects. Other comments in the same issue indicated that overweight women also have other complications that lead to higher rates of complications and even death for the mothers and the unborn children.

The initial screening stage of the process may continue for weeks or even months before finding someone who seems to meet your expectations. Expect to hear the basic information on several surrogates and do not feel badly when you reject them. Wait for the person who is right for you and rest assured that many of the women you reject will be right for another couple who also is searching for a good match.

After the initial screening, the couple and the potential surrogate will review each other's personal profile(s). The British group, COTS (Childlessness Overcome Through Surrogacy), recommends that only mothers become surrogates, citing the possibility that the surrogate herself was infertile or that complications of the pregnancy or birth could render her infertile. Additionally, the need to give the first child she has borne to its genetic parents could be difficult emotionally, especially for a woman who had never given birth.

If, after reviewing each other's profiles, the surrogate and the couple both still think they could have a good working relationship, a meeting is arranged. The surrogacy program is the mediator throughout this process and arranges the meeting place and time, and also guides the discussion. Ideally, the initial meeting will be conducted in neutral territory — the program's place of business.

The first meeting between the potential surrogate and her family and the potential parents can be among the most awkward imaginable. Nervous energy often rules the day. Everyone involved attends the meeting knowing they will be judged. How do you ask a stranger to bear your child? The program coordinator is invaluable during this meeting, often asking the questions that wouldn't otherwise be broached either through lack of familiarity with the issues or politeness.

Expect the usual chit-chat while comfort levels are being established. Eventually, the conversation will turn to the matter at hand, and all the difficult questions. Expect to discuss:

- How you feel about abortion.
- Multiple births and any limits.
- Beliefs or uncertainties that could cause you to rethink your position on surrogacy.
- What the parents will tell their children about this surrogacy arrangement?
- What will you tell your extended family, and how much influence do they have on your decision?

- What you would do in the event of serious birth defects.
- Whether you are prepared for a deluge of comments regarding surrogacy.

Additionally, couples can expect to be asked why they are infertile and whether both the husband and wife are ready to commit to surrogacy.

Potential surrogates can expect to also be asked:

- How her husband feels about her being a gestational surrogate?
- Is he aware of the demands this also places upon him?
- Do you have a support network you can call on for help during this pregnancy?
- What are the differences between carrying your own child and carrying the child of another couple?
- Do you have a timeframe beyond which this arrangement would not work? (School or work schedules, for example?)
- Do you have certain requirements (religion, number of children, marital status, etc.) for the couple?

Although the urge to paint the perfect picture is strong, tell the unvarnished truth. It may take a bit longer to make the right match but the wait will be worth the effort in the long run because you will work with someone whose views, and therefore whose decisions regarding this pregnancy, are more likely to be similar to your own. It also avoids unpleasant surprises if the pregnancy goes awry. Remember, you will be working together for about one year and need the utmost trust and confidence in each other.

The questions can become quite personal, especially for the surrogate. Frequency of intercourse is an important area, because surrogacy demands a period of celibacy of about one month before she begins her medications to ensure that she is not pregnant. This infringes upon the life of the potential surrogate's husband (or significant other). The husband typically supports his wife's decision, but doesn't always understand it.

Expectations of how each party will be involved during the process preceding insemination and during the pregnancy is another important area that should be addressed now. For example:

- Do you both expect to attend every medical appointment together?
- Do you want an amniocentesis to be performed?
- Have you ever had a venereal disease?
- Will the parents be in the delivery room?
- May they film the birth?
- What happens if a Cesarean section is recommended?
- How often do you expect to talk with each other?

Another questions that must be discussed is the division of authority during the pregnancy. Regardless of any contract or any oral understanding, in the U.S., the surrogate has ultimate control because, under the U.S. Constitution, she has a right to bodily integrity and privacy. She can at any time (within legal limits) have an abortion. She also can refuse medical interventions, like amniocentesis. Nonetheless, expectations should be discussed.

There are a host of other questions that can and should be asked now, before any commitment has been made. These are the issues that can cause a great deal of difficulty during the pregnancy. It is better to refuse to work together now than to choose a surrogate or couple whose ideas and expectations clash. Legal issues aside, surrogacy is based upon a great deal of trust among all parties. The surrogate needs to trust that the couple really wants this child and to know that she is doing something that is truly valued by them. The couple must trust that the surrogate and her husband both are committed to carrying a child for them and caring for that unborn child.

Additionally, has the potential surrogate talked with women in this surrogate program? If she hasn't, she may want to sit in on a group session with their psychotherapist or meet several at various stages in the program. By meeting women who are now or have recently been gestational surrogates, the prospective surrogate can gain a better understanding of what the experience really is like. Questions may include:

- What were your expectations?
- Were they met?
- How did your couple treat you?
- How long did it take to become pregnant after agreeing to work with your couple?
- Did this pregnancy feel different than other pregnancies? If so, how?
- How did your husband and family react?
- How did you explain this to your children?
- What happened after the baby was born?
- Would you do this again, knowing what you now know?
- What makes this worthwhile for you?

- What are your biggest complaints or disappointments regarding your experience with surrogacy?

Meeting other gestational surrogates can help a prospective surrogate and her husband or boyfriend develop realistic expectations of the relationship and the surrogacy experience and help them decide whether to proceed and enter into a surrogacy relationship.

If you agree to work together, expect a few days to think it over before a firm commitment is made towards forming a surrogacy partnership. Consider inviting the surrogate to your home (at your expense) to let her see how you live and to be assured that the child would be reared in a good environment. If the idea and this particular partnership still sounds good, the process will begin with another round of testing.

This time, the surrogate, her husband or significant other, and each of the potential parents will be tested for communicable diseases, including AIDS. The surrogate, and in some programs the potential parents, should be screened by a psychologist to help identify any potential problems and to screen out candidates who seem unstable for surrogacy. The Minnesota Multiphasic Personality Inventory is just one of the tests that may be administered. This step occurs very early in some programs, before a couple is identified for the surrogate, and sometimes after they have met and agreed to work together, pending the outcome of all of the tests. (Consider this screening an opportunity to avoid lawsuits before they can occur.) At the least, the prospective parents should talk with the psychologist to gain a better understanding of the psychological aspects of surrogacy.

The meeting with the psychologist offers a good opportunity to gain insights regarding surrogates' perspectives as their pregnancies progress and on more specific ways to provide emotional support to the surrogate, how other surrogacy relationships have been played out, what you can do to make this relationship as smooth as possible for all concerned and how to end the relationship once the baby is born, if that is what both parties wish to do. Typically, couples will be provided with a psychological profile of the surrogate, based upon her scores in standard psychological tests. That survey is based upon a personal interview with the psychologist and upon tests results, and may restate much of the information that is outlined by the surrogate herself in the personality profile. It will include the psychologist's recommendation regarding her acceptability as a surrogate.

Be aware, however, that although there have been studies of women who became surrogates, there is, as yet, little data about what makes a good surrogate. If the results are satisfactory, the couple and the surrogate will meet with an infertility specialist and begin a medical regimen that, hopefully, will result in pregnancy.

Throughout this early stage, stay in touch with your surrogate. An occasional card to say hello or an invitation to a picnic or some other casual event during this time will help to reinforce your interest in her well-being and your gratitude for what she is trying to do, and also helps you all get better acquainted before the pregnancy begins.

8   Contracts

Contracts for surrogacy — including contracts with the surrogate and with a surrogate program — are not legal in all U.S. states or in all nations. But, in many states and nations, there are not laws specifically mentioning surrogacy. In others, laws are very specific regarding surrogacy and surrogacy requirements (Chapter 4). If surrogacy contracts are not illegal, you should have written agreements with all parties to minimize misunderstandings. This chapter provides an overview of what should be included in such contracts, and the number and type of contracts that you may expect in areas where surrogacy is not illegal.

Contract clauses in this chapter are based upon California law. Laws in your area will differ. Consult with your attorney before drawing or signing any contracts.

Program Contract

The first contract you will sign is an agreement with a surrogacy program to provide specified services. The agreement remains in effect until the surrogate returns all parental rights to the natural parents. The program's services should be specified as well as the couple's rights and obligations regarding those services. The natural parents should have the right to refuse any or all surrogates for any reason, although there may be a rematching fee after a certain number of attempted matches. The program should agree to provide regular emotional support and encouragement throughout the duration of the surrogacy agreement for both the surrogate and the couple. That includes ensuring that the surrogate has her own attorney (paid for by the couple) before signing the surrogate agreement, a physical exam before the agreement is signed, health insurance and life insurance before the embryo transfer occurs, throughout the pregnancy and for a reasonable time afterwards, and mental health counseling during the pregnancy and for several months afterward.

The contracts should cause the surrogacy program to provide written information about the surrogate, including her medical history and personality. The program should help ensure that the surrogate is covered under insurance for the costs of the prenatal care and delivery or notify the potential parents that insurance is lacking. The surrogacy program also should agree to provide an accounting to the prospective parents of the surrogate's expenses incurred on their behalf, which are to be paid from a trust fund or escrow account established for this purpose by the prospective parents.

Furthermore, the contract may stipulate that the fee paid to the program is not refundable if the program complies with the terms of the contract, regardless of whether a child is born from the surrogacy arrangement. The contract also should specify the fees if the prospective parents try to have another child with the same surrogate and if they chose to work with a different surrogate.

Pay particular attention to the wording in the contract regarding the protection of privacy. Some contracts specify that the agreement will be confidential and not mentioned to any third party. That could make it rather difficult to explain to your friends and relatives exactly where this child came from and how it happens to be yours. What is more common is to agree not to publicize the names of the surrogate, the prospective parents and sometimes the surrogacy program without their express written consent.

The contract also should call for the formation of an escrow account or trust fund. The account should have sufficient funds to pay medical fees, insurance premiums, the surrogate's expenses, attorneys' fees, and the fees of all other professionals associated with the surrogacy agreements. Expect to deposit about $30,000 into this account in one lump sum and to receive a monthly accounting, and to add funds to the account, for a total of about $40,000. The account may be established and held by your attorney, a bank or an escrow office like those used to handle real estate transactions in some states.

It is important to note that a surrogacy program is not a one-stop shopping center. Although it may or may not find a surrogate, depending upon local law, it should help screen the surrogate and provide a great deal of guidance. The program will not provide medical advice or guarantee that a child will result from this arrangement or that the child will be healthy and free of any birth defects. Although some surrogacy agencies have an attorney on staff to provide legal advice, not all do so.

The Psychotherapist

Expect to sign a contract with a psychotherapist to provide an evaluation for your surrogate and to provide group or individual counseling sessions. Typically, the agreement stipulates that the surrogate is the patient of the psychotherapist and that charges incurred by the surrogate that relate to surrogacy will be paid by the prospective parents. In the contract, the psychotherapist should agree to provide a written evaluation of the potential surrogate, ongoing counseling during the pregnancy and for a few months afterward, and provide for consultations with the surrogacy program and a meeting with the prospective parents, monthly group therapy sessions for the surrogate, individual therapy sessions as needed, a termination clause and a contingency to provide services for a second surrogate if the first is unacceptable or drops out of the program for any reason. Note that some areas also require an initial screening for the couples, as well as the surrogate.

Surrogate Contract

In addition to the contract with the surrogacy program, you also will sign a contract with the surrogate that spells out the purpose of the agreement as well as the details associated with achieving its goal. Contracts will vary according to program and state or nation. This contract should state the facts of the arrangement: the prospective parents are married and are living together, the prospective mother is medically unable to carry a pregnancy safely to term, all parties are of legal age and are making an informed decision voluntarily, the surrogate's husband (if any) supports this arrangement, the surrogate believes that both morally and contractually, the child is that of the prospective parents, the surrogate desires no parental relationship with it and that the surrogate believes herself to be capable of bearing healthy children. The contract should briefly outline the pertinent medical details that define gestational surrogacy.

The surrogacy contract should stipulate that the surrogate will follow the medical advice provided by her physician in regards to prenatal care, including abstaining from caffeinated beverages, non-prescribed drugs, alcohol and any activities that could be dangerous to the child she will carry. A clause outlining when abortion, selective reduction or amniocentesis may be permissible also should be included. Typically, the surrogate would only choose an abortion to preserve her own health, but the U.S. Constitution grants her that right regardless of the terms of any contract. The genetic parents could opt for abortion if the physician determined that the child would have severe physical or physiological abnormalities, but the final decision is the surrogate's. Financial obligations in the event of a miscarriage also should be specified.

The contract also should identify the state and country in which the child is to be born. Because of the laws in the U.S., this is an important detail. Talk with your attorney about the possibility of also including a clause specifying any states or nations the surrogate should avoid during the late stages of the pregnancy. The reason for these precautions is that if the child is born in a state that does not recognize surrogacy, the contract may be unenforceable and all parental rights and legal authority for the child may belong to the surrogate. In a best-case scenario, that merely increases paperwork and travel distances while the child and surrogate are hospitalized. In a worst case situation, the genetic parents and the surrogate may face imprisonment and substantial fines, depending upon the state. This point is worth discussing with the surrogate to ensure that she understands the rationale behind that statement and its importance to her own safety as well as to her couple's.

The contract also should have an escape clause for the surrogate and for the couple, specifying under what situations and until what event either party can void this contract, as well as specifying rights of all parties if one party breaches the contract. Also, confidential information will remain confidential. In states or nations that recognize the genetic parents as the child's parents from the time of birth, the contract should stipulate that the genetic parents are financially responsible for their child regardless of any physiological problems, and should require wills to care for the child in the event of the genetic parents' death before the child is born. The contract should require the surrogate and her husband to sign legal and medical "informed consent" forms. The contract also should specify that the genetic parents, the surrogate and her husband or partner are free of certain communicable diseases, including AIDS.

Additionally, the contract should reiterate the status of the law regarding surrogacy and abortion, and indicate that no warranties can be made regarding the ultimate cost or liability for each of the parties, or their obligations.

The contract should specify that the genetic parents are the legal parents of any child or children born because of this agreement and that they will take all financial and medical responsibility for that child or children, even if congenital abnormalities or defects are present. If legal in your area, the contract also should specify that the surrogate will relinquish all parental rights to the child upon its birth. Otherwise, it may specify the terms under which the child will become the responsibility of its genetic parents, according to the law in your area.

Be careful that the terms of reimbursement for the surrogate are spelled out in the contract and that the sums are considered reimbursements for her expenses during the pregnancy and delivery. If the contract indicates that money is to be paid in exchange for delivering a baby to the commissioning couple, the contract may be considered invalid and the surrogate, the genetic parents and other parties to the transaction may be charged with baby-selling/buying and, as a consequence, face criminal penalties. Ensure that your surrogacy contract cannot be construed in that light.

The willingness of the surrogate and her husband to undergo psychological screening and, if needed, counseling also should be specified. The surrogate and her husband or significant other should give the psychologist the freedom to discuss their counseling and evaluation with the prospective parents where it relates to the surrogacy situation. Medical testing for the surrogate and the prospective parents should be specified. The surrogate also should agree not to have sexual intercourse (or any other activity that could introduce semen into her body) for a specified period. If the prospective parents opt for sex selection, the surrogate should not object to the procedure, although it has no bearing on the surrogacy agreement. The surrogate, however, has the right to object to any physically invasive procedure. The surrogacy agreement can be terminated by a physician if a pregnancy has not occurred within a reasonable time. You should discuss with the surrogacy program and with the infertility specialist what "a reasonable time" is, and put it in writing before signing the agreement.

Depending upon state law, the surrogate may be responsible for her own child care arrangements and expenditures. Reimbursement for any lost wages that result from this agreement also depends upon state law.

Life insurance policies should be taken out in a specified amount for both of the natural parents, which names the child as a beneficiary, and for the surrogate. The policies are to remain in effect until the agreement terminates for the couple, and for at least six weeks after the agreement terminates for the surrogate. Insurance brokers who specialize in life insurance are available. Check your local phone book for listings.

9 Expenses and Logistics

One of the first big questions for potential parents in this endeavor may be finances. Surrogacy is not an inexpensive proposition, and it costs more than most media accounts lead one to believe. Virtually none of it is tax deductible. It's not necessary for potential parents to be wealthy, but it does help to have liquid assets. Costs are incurred in several areas and from several different sources, so even your surrogacy program may be unable to provide more than an estimate of overall expenses. Additionally, costs will vary according to the program you choose, the fertility specialist, the number of attempts with the specialist before pregnancy results, your choice of attorney or other escrow holder, changes to your will, whether the surrogate is insured, whether your insurance will cover in vitro fertilization and whether any special medical services are needed immediately after the child is born. Also, because the possibility of multiples is more likely, the risk of premature birth also increases and, with it, the possibility of medical costs of hundreds of thousands of dollars. Where you live also will affect costs, because costs for the same treatment at the same type of medical facility varies widely throughout the U.S.

Note that U.S. tax changes adopted in 1996 under the Minimum-Wage Law do not apply to any adoptions undertaken as a result of surrogacy because they are viewed as adopting the child of your spouse.

1992 Surrogacy Costs

Surrogacy program	$ 9,000
Surrogate's expenses	13,500
($3,000 bonus for twins; $5,000 for triplets)	
Fertility clinic	8,000
Medications	1,500
New wills	350
Psychologist	3,000
Dietitian	55
Life insurance (for surrogate)	200
Health insurance (surrogate)	1,560
Life insurance (for couple)	300
Attorney fees for parents'	3,000
Surrogate's attorney	1,000
Hospital delivery	8,000
(when not covered by insurance)	
Pager, if desired	300
Total Cost:	**$49,765**

Medications are one of the big expenses that often are out-of-pocket. Costs can vary considerably, depending upon the medications and where they are acquired. Check with your fertility clinic and fertility specialist, several pharmacies in several nations, pharmaceutical supply houses and infertility support groups for sources of low-cost medications.

Out-of-country pharmacies also may supply the medications from your prescription, using overnight mails and credit card purchasing. Check with your infertility specialist for sources, or access the Internet. Ascertain that the strengths of the medications match your prescription. If you use this method, phone the Food and Drug Administration (FDA) to ascertain the quantities of the medications you can order from abroad, and allow extra time in case the medications are delayed by customs authorities.

Costs for the fertility clinic vary widely. You can expect costs for one IVF cycle to range between $4,500 and $15,000, including ultrasounds, lab fees, anesthesia, aspiration of the oocytes, embryo transfer and normal lab tests, as well as professional and technical fees. Costs and quality of treatment are not related, so you will find that some — but not all — of the lower cost programs also are the most successful. Medications are extra and may cost another $2,000 per cycle. You may be able to reduce the medication costs by shopping carefully for discount pharmacies, and by asking whether unopened medications can be returned for a refund. Ask the clinic for a fee schedule and an explanation of which treatment you will be given.

Costs for the surrogate are broken down, for example, to $525 per month for partial reimbursement of rent or mortgage, $385 per month for partial payment of food expenses and $140 per month for partial payment of clothing expenses. The exact breakdown of costs will vary according to state or national law, and reimbursement for expenses that would have been incurred regardless of pregnancy may not be allowed. Those payments begin once pregnancy is confirmed and will continue through the pregnancy and for a specified recovery period afterwards. Medical and travel expenses also will be reimbursed during the period preceding the embryo transfer. The actual amounts will vary with the program.

The psychotherapist will provide testing and an evaluation of the surrogate carrier applicant and a written report. The dietitian will meet with the surrogate once to provide dietary recommendations and will be available to answer questions — for example, ways to minimize morning sickness — throughout the pregnancy. These expenses may be paid up-front, in lump sums or paid through an escrow account.

Wills

By the time the oocytes are aspirated, you should have new wills written, signed and in your files. If you don't have an attorney, you may want to choose one who is familiar both with estate planning and surrogacy, but it isn't necessary. Just explain the procedure in detail so the attorney is left with no doubt regarding the origin of the genetic material that must be provided for. Specifically, your new wills should:

- Provide for the disposition of unfertilized oocytes if the husband, wife or both are deceased.

- Provide for the disposition of any embryos, either cryopreserved or awaiting implantation if the husband, wife or both are deceased.

- Provide for the child carried by the surrogate if both genetic parents are deceased.

- Ensure that any reimbursements that are stipulated in the surrogacy contract are honored by your estates.

You also may want to include a section discussing the rights of inheritance of any sperm, oocytes or embryos that are not yet implanted at the time of your demise, as well as the rights of inheritance of any fetuses at that time.

For example, if the husband dies, may the wife have embryos that were conceived with him implanted into a surrogate after his death and, if so, may they inherit any portion of his estate? Likewise, if the wife dies, may the husband fertilize the waiting oocytes and have them implanted? May they inherit any portion of the wife's estate? May you stipulate a time-frame beyond which the embryos may not be implanted? To further complicate the issue, some states forbid the willful destruction of human embryos. Therefore, if you die and still have 12 frozen embryos what can your estate do?

Insurance

Infertility treatments may be covered. According to a benefits summary compiled by the National Association of Insurance Commissioners in 1995, coverage for infertility treatment is mandated in 12 states, with mandated offerings or mandated with limitations in six others. See Appendix D for a list of states with mandated coverage for infertility treatments. Your fertility clinic may work with several insurers and may even have preferred provider arrangements with them or with health maintenance organizations or preferred provider organizations. Do not assume, that you will be covered for IVF or surrogacy if you are a member of one of those plans. Every policy is different.

Even with mandated coverage for infertility treatments, however, treatments involving surrogacy may not be covered. For example, embryo transfer may not be covered even though the medical care leading up to the transfer was covered. This is a gray area for most insurers, including self-insured companies, and no research has been conducted by the industry on the topic.

Some clinics require a letter of authorization from your insurer for each cycle of treatment. That letter will specify the patient's name, identification number, group number, the percentage of fees to be reimbursed, the number of attempts allowed, and whether there is a lifetime maximum. Check for your clinic's individual requirements.

Maternity coverage is mandated in six states and is mandated with limitations on coverage or is mandated to be offered in seven states. However, companies will not reimburse expenses for prenatal care or delivery unless the person giving birth is covered for that care under one of its policies. The argument that you would be pregnant yourself if it were possible is irrelevant to the insurer.

Unless a surrogate is already insured, it may be difficult — if not impossible — to find an insurance plan and have her enrolled and eligible to receive benefits before the embryo transfer occurs. When you first contract with a surrogate program, begin researching insurance firms. Many surrogates will be uninsured. The surrogate program may be able to recommend some plans, but don't count on it. The simplest method is to contact a health insurance broker and also to contact managed care providers (health maintenance organizations, preferred provider organizations and independent physician associations) in your area.

When shopping for health plans for your surrogate, even if you haven't found a surrogate yet, ascertain whether the plan has a waiting period before maternity benefits may be used and, if so, its duration. Three months is not uncommon. That will determine when fertility treatments for the surrogate and the genetic mother may begin. Ask for a current benefits book, and also ask about:

- The duration of the waiting period before maternity benefits can be used.

- Which hospitals accept this plan.

- Whether the plan covers medically necessary transfers

to tertiary care medical facilities.
- What happens if the delivery occurs at a hospital not participating in this plan.
- Costs.
- Enrollment periods.
- Whether a medical exam is necessary.
- Why the plan would refuse enrollment.

Although Kaiser Permanente and Blue Cross/Blue Shield indicated that surrogacy was not an issue that affected medical coverage of their clients, not all plans take that attitude and not all plans within the same insurer approach surrogacy the same. Policies may change over time. Remember, seeking to insure a surrogate is no different than a couple seeking maternity coverage because they are planning a family. The key difference is that a surrogate typically will be covered for one to two years and the young family may stay with the plan longer.

Surrogate programs still report problems with insurers once they learn the pregnancy is a surrogacy situation. Medicaid and Champus (military insurance), for example, will not cover surrogacy situations. There is some debate among surrogacy agencies, surrogates and prospective parents about ascertaining whether a policy reimburses surrogate pregnancies. The fear is that once a firm is alerted to surrogacy, anti-surrogacy clauses may be inserted. The best assurance is to request a copy of their current benefits booklet and refer to it before embarking upon surrogacy and to ensure that it is current before the embryo transfer occurs. Keep the booklet. You may need it later to prove that surrogacy was not exempted from your coverage plan at the time of the delivery.

Unless the policy specifies that surrogacy situations are not covered, insurers are legally bound to fulfill their obligations as outlined in the coverage policy. However, surrogate agencies report that a few insurance companies are beginning to insert "no surrogacy" clauses into their policies. Currently, insurance industry associations are not tracking policy coverage in surrogacy situations and individual companies say either that surrogacy is not an issue or that it depends upon the individual plan. Remember, this is a new phenomena for the insurance industry, too, and most insurers simply haven't thought about it.

Insurers say they have no way of knowing whether a woman is a surrogate. Oftentimes, surrogacy will not be noticed unless it is clearly marked in the files and, depending upon the insurer, it may not become an issue even then. With Champus (military) insurance, that notification means the genetic parents pay any outstanding claims related to the pregnancy or delivery. At Medicaid, the feeling is that Medicaid is a payer of last resort and that if a surrogacy contract existed, the contracting couple would be legally obligated to pay the costs associated with prenatal care and the birth and hospitalization of the surrogate. There are no guidelines addressing this, however. Generally, if an insurer doesn't audit the medical files, the surrogacy component of the birth will go unnoticed and so claims will be paid.

The Self Insurance Institute of America had no guidelines for its members regarding surrogacy. Self-insured companies are exempt from state laws governing insurance and so are exempt from any coverage mandates. They tend to offer policies that are similar to those of commercial insurance carriers. Many of these companies hire outside firms to conduct utilization review — a review of health care resources and billing — to help ensure that billing is accurate and that any proposed treatments are necessary. Audits also may be conducted after the fact. In that situation, an auditor may notice that there was no follow-up care for the child (because upon birth it is covered by its genetic parents' policy) and may flag the file. The effect upon coverage depends upon the individual carrier. The notification in the file that the birth mother is a surrogate also may trigger attention. Options for the insurer are to ask for full or partial reimbursement up to that point or to cover the claim anyway. Trends in that area have not been tracked by the insurance industry.

If payment is requested, it is most likely to be for any outstanding claims — probably hospitalization and delivery. The rationale is that a contract was signed specifying a child's conception and providing for its prenatal care, thus making this a business in which health care expenses are the major cost of conducting business. The insurer has no interest in subsidizing the business of surrogacy.

The most likely time for surrogacy to be noticed is immediately before or after the birth of the child simply because a note indicating that this is a surrogacy situation is likely to be added to the file at that point to ensure that the proper name is entered on the birth certificate and that the genetic parents are accorded parental rights if any treatments are needed for the child. If the surrogate is a member of a plan that may question medical claims based upon surrogacy, it could be worthwhile to buy another medical plan for the duration of the surrogacy relationship and for a few months afterward, as specified in the surrogacy contract. Supplemental insurance, such as in-hospital indemnity plans, offers another form of insurance, but not all states allow its use in surrogacy situations.

The Obstetrician

Not all obstetricians are willing to work with surrogate pregnancies. Some will be delighted and a large group will be curious. You may find your best experience is with an obstetrician recommended by the fertility specialist, simply because of familiarity with surrogacy partnerships. Whomever you choose, ensure that the choice is made jointly by the surrogate and the prospective mom (assuming you both are in the same geographic area). After all, both the pregnant surrogate and the expectant mom must be comfortable with the physician and staff, and the office location should be convenient for both. It also should offer hours that allow both the expectant mom and the surrogate to attend the medical appointments, and should accept the surrogate's insurance plans or be willing to make the appropriate financial arrangements with the expectant parents. Importantly, ensure that the physician is on staff at a hospital that accepts both your medical plan and that of the surrogate. If the pregnancy is considered high risk, you also may need to ensure that the obstetrician is on staff at a hospital with a neonatal intensive care unit (ICU) and that that hospital accepts both insurance plans.

The Hospital

Typically, you would select a hospital near home. Working with a surrogate complicates this. You must find a hospital that accepts the surrogate's insurance for the delivery and the parents' insurance for care after birth, and you need a hospital that is convenient for the surrogate. If the pregnancy is considered high risk, either because of medical complications or because the surrogate is carrying multiples, you also will want to ensure that the hospital has a neonatal intensive care unit. At least identify such a hospital for a transfer in case it is needed. Additionally, you must find a hospital with a nursing staff that is comfortable with surrogacy and whose bureaucracy can accommodate your situation easily.

Before choosing a hospital, talk with a social worker or patient advocate, the nursing director and possibly the chief of obstetrics at hospitals you are considering to discuss the hospital's capabilities and the surrogacy situation specifically. Ask whether the hospital is familiar with surrogate births, whether its staff is comfortable dealing with them and how surrogate births there may differ from other births in terms of care for the surrogate and issues regarding the child.

If the hospital is unaware of the situation by the time of birth, the nursing staff may be concerned that the surrogate — whom the nurses presume to be the mother — is not bonding with the baby and may put additional pressure upon her. Additionally, the hospital may allow only family into the delivery room – thus eliminating the child's parents. To help avoid such awkward situations, talk with several hospitals several months before the birth and then choose the one that best meets your criteria. Some hospitals have suggested getting their policies in writing, so all parties understand the details of the hospital's involvement.

Gestational surrogacy often is confused with traditional surrogacy — even among hospital personnel. Because of that confusion, the maternity and nursery nurses are likely to refer to the surrogate as the mother and to assume that the genetic parents must adopt the child. Regardless of their beliefs, the surrogate will be regarded as the legal parent until legal documents specify otherwise. Physicians and nurses will be legally bound to turn to the surrogate for all questions concerning the baby, the baby's medical treatment and the baby's insurance coverage.

Once the hospital has legal proof that you are the parents, there still may be some confusion. Hospital staff may refer to the child using the surrogate's last name rather than the last name of the genetic parents and, at first, may continue to ask her wishes on medical advice. Also, even with the court order on file, the birth certificate may have the surrogate's name as the mother, or a combination of the names of the surrogate and the genetic parents and even a combination of their addresses.

The fact that this is a surrogate delivery makes this birth a special case and can cause enormous frustration for the parents and the surrogate if the hospital is not prepared to deal with surrogate births. Even if the hospital has some experience in this area, glitches can occur easily. Questions include:

- How many surrogate births have occurred here?
- How and when do they prefer to be notified of an impending surrogate birth?
- May you all attend childbirth classes?
- May you tour their facility?
- Will the genetic parents be allowed in the delivery room?
- After the birth, will the surrogate be returned to the maternity ward or to a general ward?
- Will the parents and the surrogate be allowed to visit the baby?
- Will the hospital show the parents how to feed and bathe the baby?
- Are there special skills parents must demonstrate, such as infant CPR, before taking the baby home?
- If so, does the hospital teach these skills?
- How long must a healthy child stay in the hospital?
- Will the baby initially be identified as belonging to the genetic parents, the surrogate or identified to both?

- Do you have a contact who serves as patient advocate, to help smooth the hospital bureaucracy?
- When will the hospital need the court order that specifies the identity of the child's parents?
- To whom should this order be given?
- How will the nursing staff be apprised of the parent's identities to ensure that the parents are accorded parental rights while the child is in the hospital?
- Will the genetic parents automatically assume medical responsibility for the child or will the staff ask the surrogate to make those decisions?
- Particularly if the hospital is affiliated with a religious organization, how are the staff members likely to respond to a surrogate birth?
- If insurance does not cover the hospital bills, what discount will the hospital provide for a cash payment? It is not unusual for the hospital and physician to reduce the bill by 25-33%.
- Will the hospital put its discount policy and percentage in writing?

The hospital may not have answers to many of those questions because gestational surrogacy is a relatively recent development and most hospitals have never dealt with the situation. Be prepared to educate the hospital staff about surrogacy and the related details that involve them. Even large, regional medical facilities that have had several surrogate deliveries simply have not developed policies because it's relatively uncommon, even in the regions where surrogacy is strong. Actual practices are wide-ranging, depending upon the state laws, the hospital's own policies and bureaucracy and the nursing staff.

At Long Beach Memorial Hospital in California, surrogates typically recover in a ward dedicated to gynecologic patients rather than in the maternity ward, and the genetic parents are welcome in the delivery room if the surrogate approves. There, surrogacy is handled on a case-by-case basis that is governed by the relationship between the surrogate and the couple and their joint wishes. The same is true at Kaiser Permanente's hospitals. Kaiser's spokesman said that common sense should prevail. Even if your hospital has such a liberal policy regarding surrogacy, expect glitches and frustrations.

Home Births

It is possible, of course, to arrange for a home delivery with a nurse-midwife (if it is legal in your state), or birth at a maternity center with a nurse-midwife or a lay-midwife, but only if the pregnancy is normal. High risk pregnancies – including multiple births – must be attended by physicians in a hospital. Surrogacy program coordinators generally advise using a hospital for a surrogate birth to minimize the risk and the liability of each of the parties in case anything goes wrong during the delivery.

Nurse-midwifes are nurses who have completed an accredited educational curriculum in nurse-midwifery and have passed a standardized exam administered by the American College of Nurse-Midwives. They are licensed and are recognized in all 50 U.S. states and by some insurance carriers. In contrast, lay midwives are not nurses and do not have formal university training in childbirth but entered the profession by apprenticeship. In many states, lay midwives are illegal, although they may be members of the Midwives' Alliance of North America and may be certified by the North American Registry of Midwives.

Studies show that babies born with midwives in attendance are as healthy as babies born in hospitals with a physician in attendance — unless there are complications. Then, a home birth can delay medical care and can result in severe or fatal complications for the child and for the woman giving birth.

A nurse-midwife can provide prenatal and postnatal care and information including nutrition, exercise, infant feeding and childbirth methods. During labor she will monitor its progression, provide pain medication or anesthesia if either is desired and also will suggest other ways to lessen the discomfort. During the delivery, the midwife will assist, and a nurse-midwife can perform an episiotomy if one is needed. Nurse-midwives also can perform such gynecological services as PAP smears, pelvic exams and breast exams, and can offer health care advice. According to midwives, the benefits of their services include more extensive prenatal visits than are usual with obstetricians, the ability to intimately involve family and friends in the birthing process, the lack of unnecessary medical interventions in a natural process, the undivided attention of the midwife during labor and delivery and expenses that can be about one fifth of the cost of a traditional hospital delivery. In some states, nurse-midwifery services are reimbursed by insurance carriers, but be certain to check with your carrier and with your surrogate's carrier to ensure coverage if you choose this route.

After the birth and for the first several days, a midwife may be legally required to attend to the surrogate and the child. Her obligations are governed by local law. Because the child and the surrogate will have different addresses, expect a lot of questions and, possibly, a visit by a representative of the local Department of Social Services. If you are interested in exploring the home-birth option, check the laws in your state, and with your obstetrician as well as with several midwives to understand exactly what to expect and how surrogacy affects that situation.

When interviewing midwives, ask:

- Whether they are comfortable with surrogacy situations.
- How many births they have attended as the midwife in charge.
- The number of live births without complications.
- Their rate of complications and still births.
- Whether they have a relationship with an obstetrician if an emergency arises.
- Whether they are nurse-midwives or lay-midwives.
- Whether they are accredited and by whom.
- Whether they are licensed.
- Whether they are comfortable with home births or prefer maternity center births.
- Whether insurance carriers cover their services.

The Court Order

One of the most important things you can do before the baby arrives is to obtain a court order specifying that the child belongs to the prospective parents and not to the surrogate. This is done as a matter of course in California, but may not be possible in other states or nations, depending upon their laws. If it is to be done, the surrogacy program coordinator and the attorney can handle this detail.

A court order, in California, is actually a series of documents, including a "complaint to declare existence of maternity and paternity," a "judgment of the parent's attorney," a "declaration for the fertility specialist," a "stipulation for entry of judgment" (agreed to by the surrogate and the prospective parents) and a "judgment of maternity and paternity" from the superior court judge (Appendix E). The wording of these documents refers to plaintiffs and defendants but, in reality, the surrogate and prospective parents have already agreed to everything specified by these documents. They are just the final formality needed to legally award custody and all financial and other responsibility to the natural parents.

Ensure that you have this document in your hands, with copies at the surrogacy program and at the hospital by the earliest time in the pregnancy that the child could be born and still live (about 22 weeks after conception). Typically, the surrogate will tell the nurse to do whatever the parents deem best, but if their opinions differ, the surrogate has the law and the hospital behind her until the court order arrives. It's a good idea for each parent to carry a copy of this order at all times during the final months of the pregnancy so that whenever labor occurs, they can meet the surrogate at the hospital with only a moment's notice and be able to legally prove to the hospital that the child is theirs. This has nothing to do with the surrogate's intentions toward the child and everything to do with the letter of the law. The physicians and hospital must follow the law and, even though all know this is a surrogacy situation and may even see copies of the surrogacy agreement, the only package of documents that will affect the legal determination of parenthood is the court order.

If the child is delivered at full term, you will just be ready early. However, if the child is premature, this will make a significant difference in the speed at which your child can receive non-emergency medical attention and in how you are treated at the hospital until the child can go home. Note that multiple births typically are premature (usually about six weeks for twins, but often earlier).

Not having the court order at the time of birth means that the hospital will consider the surrogate as the legal mother and will require her to make any medical decisions, including circumcision, that should be made by the baby's parents. Even when the physicians and nurses understand the situation and are sympathetic and the parents are standing next to them, if a medical decision must be made that requires the parents' input, the nurse must, by law, contact the surrogate for her decision.

If the child is born before you have a court order specifying you as the parents, the child will be listed under the surrogate's last name. When the court order arrives, the name should be changed, but it often takes several weeks for the hospital to do this. Reasons range from bureaucratic paperwork to the fact that the nurses all are familiar with the baby or babies under the surrogate's name and are loathe to change it. It also means that the baby's birth certificate is likely to be issued in the wrong name and must be amended. The birth certificate cannot be issued without the mother's signature, but mistakes still occur and the hospital may try to pressure the surrogate to sign the certificate. Make certain you talk with a hospital social worker about this situation so you at least can prevent the birth certificate from being issued until you have the court order and so can have the certificate issued using the genetic parents' names.

In areas other than California, you may be able to obtain a court order listing the genetic father as the baby's father and giving him parental rights. The genetic mother may need to complete a step-parent adoption. Check with your attorney to determine the best procedures for your state or nation.

10   Managing Expectations

You probably won't have a perfect match between a couple and a surrogate, but you can get very, very close. That is one reason it is worth the extra time to wait until you meet someone you like and whose judgment you can fully trust during the pregnancy. For example, that may mean choosing someone who doesn't smoke or drink, who exercises, who eats a balanced diet, and who exhibits a healthy judgment. That doesn't mean you necessarily approve of each of the other's life decisions, but that you respect each other and believe you each can be a good parent. The more similar you are, the easier this can be.

When a surrogacy relationship first forms, some prospective parents will want to be involved with the surrogate as much as possible — attending every medical appointment and having close, frequent contact. Others want a neat, clean business arrangement, with little personal contact. The reality, according to surrogate program coordinators, is that regardless of a couple's stated intentions, once they get to know the surrogate they tend to want to be as closely involved in this pregnancy as possible. The surrogate and the prospective mom will have their own, separate appointments with the fertility specialist and, in fact, could complete the pregnancy without ever meeting again. However, by the time of the embryo transfer, you probably are becoming friends and will want to share the experience.

You may want to discuss how you want to be told you're expecting — and also how to be told that you're not. Sometimes the clinic is in charge of news, phoning either the surrogate or the intended parents. Other times the surrogate program delivers the news. Some couples prefer that the wife be told before the husband, letting them duplicate the more usual experience. Sometimes it's a gradual process of going to appointments and knowing the embryos were transferred and implanted and are growing. How you hear the news — and from whom — is up to you, but if you have a script in mind, plan now to help accomplish it.

Surrogacy agencies say that relationships between the surrogate and the couple tend to be friendly, sometimes almost like family. If you live or work in the same area, during the course of the pregnancy you tend to meet each other often and have some telephone contact. If you are geographically distant, you still can share information by phone, fax, e-mail and mail. By the time a baby is born, many parents commonly refer to their surrogate as an angel and the child as a miracle baby.

Usually, by the time a pregnancy is confirmed, the surrogate and the couple have formed a closer relationship and the surrogate may be determined that the couple's — or at least the mom's — experience of expecting the baby will be as close to pregnancy as possible. So, moms who treat their surrogate's pregnancy as if it was their own, by attending all of the medical appointments with the surrogate, even when they're not convenient, gain some additional respect from the surrogate and also gain a much better understanding of exactly what their surrogate is enduring for their sake. They also have a wonderful opportunity to see their baby's heart beat for the first time, and to watch their children grow and thrive thanks to the ultrasound examinations that are so frequent (every two weeks) at this early stage. Be sure to have the clinic videotape the ultrasound exams to share with Dad and anyone else who may care. This is especially important for parents who cannot attend medical appointments. Some couples have lived in other nations and contracted with American surrogates. They rely upon overnight mail services and electronic communications to track the pregnancy and to support their surrogate.

Once the surrogate is pregnant, ask your program to have her write a letter stating that you are the parents of her child and that the unborn child should go to you if anything happens to her in childbirth or in any accident during the pregnancy that claims her life but that allows the child to be saved. The first priority, needless to say, is to save the life of the surrogate in such an incident. If that is not possible, it sometimes is possible to save the life of the baby. The letter should be in her family's files and a copy should be with the surrogate program. Have it notarized. Because the laws are so varied throughout the U.S. and the world, this is just a practical consideration that protects the genetic parents as well as the surrogate's own family, and upholds the intent of the surrogacy contract.

Medical Concerns

An amniocentesis (which detects Down's syndrome and also identifies the sex of the child) is only one of many factors that can cause a miscarriage. Typically, it only is routinely performed with women over age 35. Discuss the risks and benefits with a genetic counselor and with your surrogate. Do you want an amniocentesis performed only if the physician recommends it or as a matter of course?

Regardless of whether an amniocentesis is performed, be prepared for a miscarriage — especially early in the pregnancy. Also, surrogates can miscarry like other women, at a rate of 5 to 10 percent, even when they follow a physician's instructions perfectly throughout the pregnancy. If a miscarriage occurs, understand that the surrogate is just as upset as you. Losing a baby is probably a new and devastating experience for her, not only because of the loss of the child but because she undoubtedly will feel that she failed you. Some surrogates have gone through this experience and have then delivered healthy children for the same couple. Others are so upset they withdraw from the program. Talk with your program coordinator about what is happening, your feelings and your surrogate's feelings, and what your next step should be. Rely upon your infertility specialist or your obstetrician for medical information. This advice also is true in the case of stillbirths and children who are born with disabilities.

Understand that a surrogacy agreement does not entitle you to a perfect child. You are not paying for a child. You are reimbursing a woman for her expenses during her attempts to become pregnant, carry a child and deliver it. Therefore, as long as the surrogate acted in good faith and heeded the medical advice provided by her physicians, she should be commended regardless of the outcome. Be kind and supportive. Help her to understand that she did everything possible to prevent a miscarriage and that you do not blame her for what happened. Remember, there is no guarantee that your child would have been born alive or in good health if you had carried the child yourself.

Obstetrical Visits

Once the pregnancy progresses to the point that the fertility specialist is no longer needed, you will be referred to an obstetrician. Visits usually are monthly for normal pregnancies. Attend these exams together whenever possible to help the physician who probably will deliver the baby to understand that you are a team. This also will remind the surrogate that you are the parents and will help you begin to bond with your unborn baby. Another benefit of attending the obstetrical visits as a team is that both you and the surrogate are more likely to be given the necessary information about the baby's development and the pregnancy's progression so neither of you hear the information second-hand.

Emotional Support

Beyond attending medical appointments together, the surrogate usually expects some emotional support from the couple. Make her feel special. Occasional notes or flowers to reassure her that she is valued can make a large impression. Phone calls just to see how she is feeling help her know that she is valued as a person and not merely as an incubator. (But remember to value her privacy and her own good judgment.) Comments to the surrogacy program that the surrogate is doing such a wonderful job are guaranteed to be passed along to her. Taking Lamaze classes with her is a good idea so you both will know better what to expect during the birthing process. The social aspect of the relationship is important to making the surrogate and her family feel valued.

For many couples, enhancing this relationship means taking the surrogate and sometimes her family to lunch or dinner, to ball games, concerts, museums, movies or other activities that she will enjoy. In California, small gifts like plants or movie tickets periodically are common. A special gift — perhaps a nice piece of jewelry — after the baby is born is considered normal. Before giving any gifts, consult with your attorney. Legally, gifts to the surrogate could cause problems. Depending upon the law in your area, a gift may be considered compensation or coercion and may put the surrogacy agreement into question. Be very careful where gifts are concerned.

The best way to emotionally support the surrogate, however, is to let her know that she is valued and her judgment is trusted. Some of the problems surrogates report are that the genetic mother somehow lets the surrogate know that she resents not carrying her child herself, and that the prospective mother is too intrusive, telling her what she should eat or how she should exercise. Another problem is that couples sometimes, even accidentally, remind the surrogate of the money involved — that they have sunk their life savings into this effort. Remember, surrogacy is an unusual situation and emotions easily may run higher than normal. A comment that may garner a laugh from a pregnant friend may be construed as meddling or considered inappropriate by a pregnant surrogate.

Also be prepared for your views or your surrogate's views to change regarding aspects of the pregnancy you had agreed upon earlier. This probably won't happen if you each are well-informed initially, but it is possible, so be prepared. For example, the genetic mom may change her mind and decide she wants an amniocentesis performed. The surrogate may decide she wants more or less contact with her couple than she at first thought. Whatever changes may occur, be logical, reasonable and friendly. Your surrogate program can discuss the changes, too — often with less emotion and more logic — and help you reach a satisfactory resolution of any differences. That is one of the benefits of working with a program.

Defining Boundaries

The division of authority regarding the pregnancy is an area where the surrogate and the couple may tussle for power. The dilemma is that it's the surrogate's body but the couple's child. Legally, the decisions are the surrogates. The best option, however, is almost always to make the decisions together and to allow the physician to have final authority regarding the medical aspects of the pregnancy. For example, if a small-framed woman is carrying triplets and the obstetrician determines that her health is being harmed and suggests selective removal of one of the fetuses, discuss it together and perhaps seek another physician's opinion but, ultimately, it is the surrogate's body and her decision. Likewise, if the child has serious birth defects, discuss the options together, but allow the genetic parents and the physicians to make the final decision, even though the surrogate (in the U.S.) has the legal authority to disregard their wishes.

In one unhappy story from San Diego, a couple contracted with a new surrogacy program. The surrogate they worked with became pregnant with triplets and was told by the physician to begin a period of bed rest. The surrogate did not follow those instructions. Upon delivery, one child required heart surgery and the other two children died. The couple is now suing, not because of the children's condition, but because the program failed to enforce the physician's instructions and because the surrogate allegedly ignored those instructions. The problem may have stemmed from poor communications and a poor choice of surrogate, but the issue of bedrest and triplets should have been discussed before the pre-embryo implantation occurred. This is why surrogacy is a matter of trust. The commissioning couple can't and shouldn't hover over the surrogate, but can encourage her to do her best. The surrogacy program coordinator, on the other hand, may command more authority and the ability to explain the consequences, as well as to act as an intermediary to solve problems before they can arise.

As a more likely, but still rare, problem, one potential surrogate announced during her first meeting with a couple that she planned to take the child home after birth to breast feed. The intent was to pass on her immunities through her milk (a noble intent) and so provide greater disease resistance to the baby. The couple was horrified. Naturally, they wanted their child home with them as soon as possible after the birth. That potential match, which had gone quite well until that point of the meeting, was never made. (Their bottle-fed child was quite healthy, as it turned out.) Offers of breast feeding have been mentioned by a few surrogacy agencies, although they add that this is quite rare. At any rate, it is one more option available to the potential parents. A more palatable option is for the surrogate to express the milk, refrigerate it and provide it to the parents, or for the genetic mother to stimulate lactation in herself. The La Leche League has information on that procedure. Infant formula also is effective.

Defining the boundaries of the surrogate/couple relationship can be uncomfortable. One couple had difficulties with a surrogate who often stopped by their home to visit and expected the couple to cancel their plans and spend the day with her. The mother-to-be eventually learned to treat the surrogate as any other friend and say "no" if the timing was inconvenient. The same issue can arise with phone calls. How much contact is too much? How much is too little? What works really depends upon the personalities of the couple and the surrogate, but cards and letters hardly can be considered intrusive, and phone calls to learn the results of specific tests are normal. If in doubt, talk to your program to learn what other people do and what this specific surrogate prefers.

A few couples have mentioned surrogates who expected them to care for their children when she or her husband were unable to do so themselves because of the requirement for bedrest after the embryo implantation or because of medical appointments. Early discussions and the contract itself should indicate that the care of the surrogate's children is her own responsibility. This is particularly true if they attend appointments with the fertility specialist. This is one of the few times the mom-to-be can be with her baby and view the ultrasound exams and hear first-hand about her child's development. The children can wait in the waiting room if they are old enough or enter the examining room with their mother without causing any problems.

Even under the best of circumstances, when everything works perfectly medically and the surrogate and her couple get along wonderfully, this is a stressful time. For the expecting parents it can be extremely difficult to relinquish the day-to-day care of their unborn child to someone else. There is a tendency to want to know that she is eating properly and exercising regularly and doing everything the parents would do to ensure a safe pregnancy and a healthy child. You need to trust that the surrogate is responsible and that she is doing her best to care for herself and your baby. Trust is a valuable commodity.

Both the surrogate and the expectant mother often are regarded as curiosities during the pregnancy. People's interest in all of the details can be quite intense and quite personal. Frankly, although some of the attention is nice, it can get old fast. For the expectant mom, sales clerks will constantly ask if she would like her baby purchases gift-wrapped or will comment, "I'd never know you were pregnant. You can't be very far along." Explaining that the baby is due next month is never the answer they expect. Neighbors, whom you may have barely met, suddenly are interested in the details — and cost — of this arrangement. Family members often may seem puzzled. Well-meaning friends and family may tell you about every fertility treatment they hear about and suggest you try it, so you won't have to work with a surrogate, and may repeat every surrogacy horror story they have ever heard. The couples' support groups that surrogacy agencies often host can help ease the pressure of feeling somehow odd and inadequate, simply because they are having similar experiences.

Be prepared for rumors that you are buying babies, even from within your own family, and be able to respond with the details, outlining the fertility treatments, embryo creation and transfer and how one unselfish women came to your aid to carry the child until you could care for it yourselves. You may need to put this in writing, in easily understood language, and circulate the explanation throughout your family.

Shortly after the birth, while the baby is still in the hospital, be prepared for comments — particularly from new fathers — about how wonderful you look, and for women who have just given birth and who want to discuss the blow-by-blow account with you and hear about your own labor and delivery. When you can't shrug off queries with, "It wasn't as difficult as I expected," or some similar comment, telling your surrogate's experience may satisfy their curiosity about the details of your child's birth. Sometimes, of course, you may simply explain that yours was a surrogate birth and watch the jaws drop. Of course, this type of discussion becomes less frequent as your child becomes older, but even years after the fact you are likely to find yourself the quiet one in a group of women telling their "war stories."

Conversely, the surrogate may be accused by her family of selling her baby. One dear lady spent her entire pregnancy explaining to her inlaws that she wasn't selling her husband's child and that no, she hadn't become involved with another man. The explanation that finally was understood was an analogy to babysitting. It wasn't her child, but she was feeding it and caring for it until it could be returned to its parents. It helped that her mother was present for the embryo transfer.

Until friends and family understand the situation, the surrogate will have to contend with the questions about why she's not buying baby things. Strangers can be brushed off with idle comments, but friends and family need to know the truth — and the sooner, the better. It's important that they understand that the child the surrogate carries has absolutely no relation to her or her husband and, therefore, to them. This is a very difficult concept for some people to understand, only partially because the ability to carry another person's child is a relatively recent phenomena. Also, it is vital that the family understand that the surrogate has her husband's support and that she and he discussed this and agreed to it long before the pregnancy occurred.

It may help to bring family and friends along gently, mentioning that you're thinking of becoming a surrogate and exploring their fears as well as her own concerns as she learns more about the process. After the birth, there will be the inevitable questions of why there's no baby in the household but, if family and friends were briefed, these questions should be only from a few people.

Briefing the Children

Many who write about surrogacy, but who have not experienced the situation themselves, fear the affect surrogacy will have on the children of the surrogate carrier. Fears include, "Will Mommy sell me or give me away?" In practice, children's reactions depend upon how the situation is explained. Clearly, don't tell children they are going to have a new brother or sister! This explanation is easiest for women who are gestational carriers and therefore have no genetic ties to the child they are carrying for another couple. Explaining the situation to the surrogate's own children actually can be easier than explaining it to adults.

Children can understand the truth, as long as the explanation is simple. For young children, "The baby's mommy can't carry her baby in her tummy, so I am helping her by carrying her baby in my tummy. When her baby is born, she and her husband will have a new baby to love and care for, just like I love you." That is a simple, easy to understand explanation that even young children can accept. As a child ages, more details may be added, but the key part is that Mommy is helping another couple by doing something that the wife couldn't do. Of course, the children may then announce to anyone who will listen that, "Mommy has a baby in her tummy, but it's not ours." To help with the explanation, the couple may provide a photograph of themselves for the surrogate to show her children, to help them galvanize the concept. After the birth, let her child see the new baby with its parents.

It's not unusual for the surrogate and her husband to discuss the possibility of becoming a surrogate with their children before the medical procedures begin and even before an agreement is reached with another couple. That way, the children helped make the decision and know what is happening from the beginning — they are aware of the plan for mommy to carry someone else's baby long before she becomes pregnant and can watch the procedure progress through the hormone shots to the day of the implantation, and then can accompany their mommy and the baby's genetic mommy to the fertility clinic and many of the subsequent appointments.

Marital Relationships

Both the parents-to-be and the surrogate and her family should expect some strains in their own relationships. The surrogate may find her husband somewhat less supportive throughout this pregnancy than earlier ones. After all, this baby is not related to him and is the result of a contractual agreement entered into by his wife. He receives no benefits — unless his wife uses her expense reimbursements for the family — and will be deprived of his wife's attentions for a period before medications begin and probably also during part of the pregnancy. Additionally, he probably will be responsible for helping his wife with her usual responsibilities to their family as her pregnancy progresses. It would be easy for even the most supportive husband to begin to resent the situation.

The parents-to-be, on the other hand, watch another woman growing large with their child. The prospective mother may watch this wonderful process and, despite her happiness as it progresses, begin to tell herself that she is "broken" or somehow incomplete. "Does my husband think of me as being less of a woman?" may be a fear of even a secure woman. And, she may be a bit jealous of the pregnant surrogate. She may need reassurances from her husband that he indeed loves her despite her perceived shortcoming, which she may feel are now evident to the world.

Even adoring husbands may feel the strain of providing constant reassurance. The husband probably will feel left out of the process and may feel that he has no control over the situation. After all, if he ever feels his child kick it won't be his wife's tummy he touches and it won't be a cozy atmosphere that encourages lingering. Because he probably won't attend the medical appointments — although attending some is recommended — most of his information is second-hand or even further removed and he can't even watch the daily progression of the pregnancy. Those feelings of isolation from the process are unlikely to go away, but they can be eased somewhat when mom and dad both are involved in the decisions in areas they can control — everything from choosing a stroller and baby clothes to decorating the nursery. And, he probably would be welcomed at medical appointments that involve ultrasound examinations. Many ultrasound machines today can make still photos as well as VHS tapes of the ultrasound, so Dad at least can view them at home the day of the exam.

Support Groups

Surrogacy certainly is becoming more common that it was a few years ago, but it's by no means an everyday occurrence. You are likely to be deluged with questions — some of them quite personal. Develop some defense mechanisms early and a constant sense of humor. You will need it.

Support groups for surrogates are vital, and they are helpful to the prospective parents as well. They alleviate the sense of isolation people can feel during the process of IVF and surrogacy and reaffirm that you're normal people in extraordinary circumstances. These groups often are the only place you can talk with others who are going through the same experience and are having the same types of fears and problems. It lets surrogates compare their experiences with those of other surrogates and to resolve problems before they become major. Couples also can compare experiences and learn new ways of dealing with uneasy situations. Contact with other couples involved with surrogacy also lets couples pool their research on such issues as insurance programs or the viability of breast feeding.

11 Ending the Relationship

The baby has just been born. The surrogate is still in the hospital. The new mom and dad want nothing more than to take their baby home and begin life as a normal family. This can be a very trying time.

The surrogate is particularly vulnerable now. Be very careful to consider her feelings and to visit her often in the hospital. It seems normal to let her see the baby and, more importantly, to see you with the baby. Help her think of you as the family she helped to create. The entire relationship has been based upon trust. Do not revoke that trust.

At its best, the relationship has been such a good partnership that it's hard to say goodbye and to realize that, under the terms of your contract you may never hear from each other again. If the baby was premature, you may find ending this relationship even more difficult than usual. You typically will spend quite a bit of time together while the surrogate is in the hospital after the delivery. For most couples and surrogates, you are trying so hard to be polite and spare each other's feelings that you may have no idea what those feelings really are. Now is a good time to talk to your program coordinator about what the surrogate really is feeling and what she really wants.

It's unrealistic to expect the relationship to end suddenly, however. The surrogate will want to see the baby a few times, for the assurance that he or she really is healthy and normal and to feel the pride of accomplishment. She also will want to see the baby with its new parents, to see with her own eyes that the child is loved and will be well cared for. After all, this woman has provided total care for the unborn child for nine months, doing everything in her power to ensure that it is healthy and that the pregnancy could be brought to term. Birth alone does not eliminate her feelings of responsibility. Countless surrogates have said that seeing the child in the parents' arms completes the circle for them and allows them to relinquish the child to its new life, and to more forward with their own lives.

If the child is premature or needs specialized care after birth, it may not be possible for the surrogate (or the new parents) to hold the child or to see parents and child together. In that case, parents can do the next best thing and videotape the interactions and then bring that tape to the surrogate's hospital room or watch the interactions through the glass. Some hospitals will allow the surrogate and the parents to visit the child in the nursery. Others may restrict access of either the surrogate or the genetic parents. Because many hospital staffs are still confused by surrogacy, talk with a social worker there to ensure that the proper people can visit your child.

For parents, this is a particularly good time to reassure the surrogate that she is still valued. Flowers, cards and other gifts are nice of course, but the best gift is a heartfelt "Thank you. You did a wonderful job and gave us our darling baby." Even if something went wrong, a surrogate who did her best for the child is still the reason that the child is as strong and healthy as it is.

The time in the hospital can be somewhat jarring for a surrogate. Nurses too often refer to her as a new mom and many hospitals keep her in the maternity wing. Despite these unwanted pressures, this is a good time for the surrogate to reassure the new parents that she is delighted for them and to begin to move forward with her own life and plans. The reassurance a surrogate gives that she feels this baby is truly her couple's is a great comfort to new parents who have read too many surrogacy horror stories to feel completely at ease, even when they had a strong relationship with their surrogate.

If you worked through a surrogacy program, the program coordinator herself can be invaluable during this weaning period between the surrogate and the couple. It's normal for the relationship to gradually lessen and for the couple and the surrogate to slowly drift apart, perhaps exchanging a card or photo annually for a year or two, reminding her of how very special she remains. Talk with your program about what the surrogate really wants and expects in terms of lessening the friendship. Telling you how other teams handle this period, and actually putting you in touch with people who have been through this stage is quite helpful. Every team handles this stage differently, and can provide their own tips and stories to prove that you will in fact separate and go on to live regular lives.

According to research by Helena Ragone, couples think of the surrogate as the woman who is carrying their child and, once the child is born, are ready to proceed as parents without her. The surrogates, Ragone found, regard the couples more as friends and generally think the relationship should continue, regardless of how well they have prepared for the relationship to end. There nearly always is a great, mutual respect between the couples and their surrogates, and also a feeling of great appreciation by the couple for their surrogate. Those feelings remain, even years after the birth. As evidence of the bond that forms, many surrogates offer to carry another child for their couple. The Center for Surrogate Parenting in Beverly Hills reports that about 20 percent of their surrogates offer to carry a second child for their couples.

One of the most common concerns during this distancing period regards what the other party is really feeling and thinking. The relationship that was built during the previous several months has just changed dramatically — the business aspect concluded with the baby's birth and the social aspect is likely to either diminish or disappear altogether. Neither wants to intrude upon the other's privacy, but both parties still may want some contact. Birth defects, prematurity or even a difficult delivery may complicate the issue. For example, the surrogate may have a difficult recovery period or the pregnancy may have affected her health or her ability to bear children, causing anguish for herself, possible recriminations from her family and friends and guilt from the couple. If the child was born with birth defects or was born prematurely, she may feel as though she failed and will need reassurance from her couple. She may not be ready for the relationship to end — particularly if the birth was much earlier than expected. In that situation, expect the social side of the relationship to continue for awhile. Phone occasionally to see how she's recovering and perhaps to ask her advice on small baby matters if she seems to want to remain somewhat involved. If you fear you may be intruding, talk to your program coordinator as an objective third party who also knows the surrogate's side of the concern. Remember, even though both the surrogate and couple initially may have agreed to cease contact after the birth , the relationship has evolved from a business arrangement into something more. The initial feelings regarding the relationship's termination may have changed.

After the birth, the surrogate, new parents and their program coordinator all may get together at the home of either the parents or the program coordinator once or twice during the first year. Sometimes the surrogate's own children will come, too, to meet and play with the baby their mom carried. A few visits are natural, and so are a few phone calls, just to know that you each are well and happy. At birthdays, holidays or anniversaries, you may exchange cards, but unless you would have been friends without meeting via the surrogacy partnership, these exchanges are likely to diminish rather quickly.

If either part of the team feels there are too many visits or phone calls, discuss the situation together. Remember, it's possible that the other truly doesn't realize the discomfort that is occurring. If the contacts still don't taper down, talk the situation over with your program director. She should be able to discuss this with either the surrogate or the new parents in a way that is non-threatening, compassionate and, most of all, objective. The voice of reason from someone who has helped many teams through this period tends to resolve the problem.

The situation is similar regardless whether the surrogate was a stranger to the couple or a close relative or friend. This is the time a new family bonds, and it's important to establish the fact that the parents and the child are the family. The surrogate's role was vital, but she has her own family to care for.

Some surrogacy programs provide opportunities for prospective and new parents to socialize, and have the surrogate enrolled in group counseling programs with other surrogates. These are good activities to continue for a while. For the new parents, the meetings can help with any surrogate separation issues that arise and allow them to show others in a similar situation that there can be a happy ending. For surrogates, the counseling sessions also bring closure to the process and help them deal with their sometimes conflicting emotions. As with the new parents, this also reminds the others in the group that the relationship will become more casual and, eventually, may end.

APPENDICES

APPENDIX A
Web Sites and Searches

The number of Internet sites with information on surrogacy and infertility is proliferating. Several surrogate agencies have home pages, and other sites devoted to health care also have information regarding agencies, surrogate selection and legislation. Because information regarding surrogacy is changing rapidly, Web searches may help provide the most current information.

If you are new to the Internet, the information in this section may help simplify your search. To conduct a search, connect to your Internet provider and enter the address of a search engine. A search engine is a tool that searches a broad portion of the Internet for specific search terms. Your provider may have a list of search engines, or you may have your own favorites. To access a search engine, select "Open URL" from the "File" menu, and enter the search engine's address. For example, http://www.lycos.com. Once you connect to that page, enter your search term and begin the Internet search.

A search term like "surrogacy" will turn up thousands of sites. To narrow your search you may want to like keywords, such as "surrogacy and California and law". Be aware that some search engines will automatically eliminate the "and", replace it with an "or" and proceed to find millions of sites that list surrogacy or California or law. Also remember that search results will vary based upon which search engine you use and upon when you conduct your search because the search engine may choose a different search pattern through the Internet and because some servers containing the information will be offline or busy. As you proceed, try changing your terms. Check "surrogate", "surrogacy", "infertility", "fertility" and other related terms and combinations of terms.

If you have an offline browser, you may want to merely collect addresses of interesting sites, send your program coordinator out to collect those sites and then visit them offline. Many search engines are available. A few of the more popular ones, with their addresses follow.

Search Engine Addresses:

AltaVista

http://altavista.digital.com

This site searches more than 21 million Web pages and also searches more than 13,000 usenet newsgroups if you check the newsgroups box when you define the search.

Excite

http://www.excite.com

This search engine searches some 1.5 million Web pages and allows searches by keyword or concept.

Lycos

http://lycos.com

Lycos includes a large number of sites with graphics, and also indexes FTP (file transfer protocol) sites. It includes 60 million URLs.

HotBot

http://www.hotbot.com

This site debuted May 1996 and automatically assumes that phrases are linked by "and", thus providing list of sites more attune to your topic.

InfoSeek Guide

http://infoseek.com

Displays are shown in order of relevance and limits search results to the first 100 hits, even though the search may reveal literally millions of hits.

OpenText

http://www.opentext.com

OpenText offers weighted searches, so you can emphasize certain words in your search term.

Inktomi

http://inktomi.berkeley.edu/query.html

This search engine that lists the number of times your search term appears in the documents it identifies as well as a page summary.

WWW Worm

http://www.cs.colorado.edu/home/mcbryan/wwww.html

This basic search engine offers 3 million URLs and lets users limit the number of returns to 5, 50, 500 or 5,000. It also lets users choose the information to display.

WebCrawler

http://www.webcrawler.com

WebCrawler, another basic search engine, displays a page's title or summary and lets users limit the number of returns to 20, 25 or 100.

Yahoo

http://spry.yahoo.com

Yahoo offers a search by category or a search of all its databases, with advanced search capabilities allowing terms such as "and" or "or" to be specified, as well as the time frames of one week, one month and three years. Titles and Web addresses are displayed without summaries.

Search.Com

http://www.search.com

Search.com contains dozens of directories and indices available for searching. The best returns appear first, and can be shown by title, title and URL, or title, URL and summary text.

Metasearches

In addition to individual search engines, you can conduct searches using metaengines. A metasearch engine searches several databases simultaneously. The best eliminate duplicate sites and combine the results on one page. Others groups and rank the best search engines for your query to form a search plan based upon its past experience and other data.

Savvysearch

http://cage.cs.colostate.edu:1969

      This performs parallel searches on up to five databases simultaneously. As many as 21 search engines are listed in order of their probable usefulness for your particular search.

All-in-One Search Page

http://www.albany,net/allinone/

      At this site, you must enter the search each time the database is changed. This site lists more than 200 basic search forms.

Internet Sleuth

http://www.intbc.comseluth/sleuth.html

      This site is designed to find specialized data and searches some 900 databases, including abstracts from the American Medical Association journals.

Internet News Groups

      There are many Internet News Groups discussing infertility and surrogacy. News groups are conversations relating to a particular topic. For example, someone will post a question and another person — or several people — will respond. The questions and responses related to each topic within the news group are called threads, and may be quite lengthy. They are hotlinked so you can read a question and click you mouse to read each subsequent response. This is not private mail. Anyone who accesses that news group can read and respond to the messages. Consequently, you are communicating with people who have personal experience with the news group's topic. Some news groups of interest are:

- news:alt.infertility
- news:misc.health.infertility
- news:alt.support.pco
- news:alt.adoption.agency
- news:alt.support.des

Other news groups may be found by searching with some of the search engines mentioned earlier, like AltaVista, and checking the "news groups" box. The following search engines concentrate solely upon news groups.

DejaNews

http://www.dejanews.com

DejaNews lets you limit searches to certain newsgroups, authors and dates.

Sift

http://sift.stanford.edu

A new feature of the Stanford Digital Library Project, this engine lets users search for topics and combine the results on a single page.

Internet Sites

American Society for Reproductive Medicine
http://www.ASRM.com

The American Surrogacy Center. Inc.
email:TASFC@surrogacy.com

http://www.surrogacy.com

This is a Web site with information regarding surrogacy and infertility.

Center for Surrogate Parenting & Egg Donation
http://www.baynet.com/surrogacy/surrpar.html

Commercial Surrogacy
http://www.gene.com/ae/AE/AEPC/WWC/1992/commercial_surrogacy.html

COTS (Childlessness Overcome Through Surrogacy)
http://www.netlink.co.uk/users/cots1

Based in the United Kingdom, COTS provides detailed information on surrogacy and IVF, and operates an infertility center.

Internet Health Resource
http://www.ihr.com

Issues in Reproductive Technology
http://Numbat.murdoch.edu.au/spermatology/spermhp.html

Physicians' list
http://www.surrogacy.com/doctor

Organization of Parents Through Surrogacy
http://www.fertilitext.ort/surrogacy.html

Surrogate Parenting Services
http://www..surrogateparenting.com

U.S. House of Representatives Master List of Web Pages
http://www.house.gov/memberWWW.html

U.S. Senate Master List of Web Pages
http://www.senate.gov/senator/members.html

APPENDIX B
Other Resources

American College of Obstetricians and Gynecologists
700 14th Street N.W., Suite 600
Washington, D.C. 20005
Phone: 202-638-5577

American Society for Reproductive Medicine
1209 Montgomery Highway
Birmingham, AL 35216
Phone: 205/978-5000
Web page: http://www.asrm.com

The Organization of Parents Through Surrogacy (OPTS)
National Headquarters
P.O. Box 213
Wheeling, IL 60090
847/394-4116
Fax:847/394-4165
Other phone numbers:

CA: 310/598-7221

NY: 212/243-0852

MA: 617/740-1783

NJ: 201/972-1181 and 201/816-9718

This national support group has several chapters throughout the U.S. It has a newsletter and maintains a legislative update.

Resolve, Inc.

1310 Broadway

Somerville, MA 02144-1731

Phone: 617/623-0744

http://www.resolve.org

This is a national support group for infertile couples and it maintains a referral list of fertility specialists, as well an extensive lending library and list of publications for sale. It also has an R.N. on staff to answer questions.

Appendix C
Surrogacy Programs

This is a partial listing of U.S. surrogacy programs. These programs have not been screened in any way in order to be listed here. Their appearance in this book is not to be construed in any way as a recommendation of their services or as a voucher of their capability. Before signing a contract with any surrogacy program, screen it thoroughly, and vigilantly monitor each step of its performance throughout the surrogacy process.

A more complete listing of surrogacy programs is available to members of the Organization of Parents Through Surrogacy, along with reports of complaints regarding specific surrogacy programs. Additional programs may be located in your local phone book or those of major cities and through database searches, such as computerized phone books. They are listed under the following U.S. government subject identification codes (SIC):

80930300 — Family Planning

93220201 — Adoption

83999900 — Social services, Miscellaneous

Adoption & Fertility Resources
144 Westwoods Drive
Liberty, MO 64068

816-781-8550

Note: Owner Kris A. Probasco, LSCSW, said her program only deals with "known" surrogates — those found by the couple — but provides the other services that are expected of surrogacy agencies. She also has an office in Overland Park, Kansas.

Center for Reproductive Alternatives of Southern California
727 Via Otono
San Clemente, CA 92672
Phone: 714-492-2161

Center for Surrogate Parenting & Egg Donation, Inc.
8383 Wilshire Blvd., Suite 750
Beverly Hills, CA 90211
Email: Centersp@AOL.com
Fax: 213-852-1310
Phone: 213-655-1974
Web: http://www.surroparenting.com

Echoes
P.O. Box 1562
Friendswood, TX 77549

Infertility Center of America
2601 Fortune Circle E., Suite 102B
Indianapolis, IN 46241
Email: noelp@nkeane.com
Fax: 317-244-3692
Phone: 317-243-8793

The Mother Goose Connection
13606 Arnold Dr., Suite #4
P.O. Box 1777
Glen Ellen, CA 95442
Email: cholmes@mgoose.com
Phone: 707-996-3062

Surrogate Mothers Inc.
P.O. Box 216
Monrovia, IN 46157
Phone: 317-996-2000 or 1-888-787-7642

Surrogate Parenting Associates, Inc.
One Medical Center Plaza
225 Abraham Flexner Way, Suite 500
Louisville, KY 40202
Email: surrogate-parenting@babies-by-levin.com
Phone: 502-584-7794

Surrogate Parenting Connection
P.O. Box 196
Alpine, CA 91903
Phone: 619/445-3733

Surrogate Parenting Services
P.O. Box 7461
Laguna Niguel, CA 92607
Phone & Fax: 714-363-9525
Email: spscristie@AOL.com

Surrogate Parents Program
11110 Ohio Avenue
Los Angeles, CA 90025
Phone: 310-473-8961

APPENDIX D
States Mandating Insurance Coverage for Infertility

This information is extracted from a chart provided by the National Association of Insurance Commissioners, which was compiled in October 1995.

Mandated Benefits for In Vitro Fertilization or other Infertility Treatments

Although insurance policies in other states may offer to cover IVF and other infertility treatments, these were the only states mandating coverage for those treatments as of October 1995, according to the National Association of Insurance Commissioners.

Arizona requires coverage of in vitro fertilization by disability insurers and sets minimum and maximum benefit levels and guidelines to determine if a policy must include IVF coverage.

California mandates that coverage for infertility treatments other than IVF be offered.

Connecticut mandates offering to groups and includes IVF.

Florida includes infertility services in its basic, preventive health care services.

Hawaii provides a one-time only benefit for outpatient IVF that applies to all group and individual health policies and hospital or medical service plan contracts and established the conditions for coverage.

Illinois mandates that group policies that cover pregnancy-related services also cover infertility and IVF services.

Maryland ensures that outpatient expenses arising from IVF cannot be excluded from health insurance policies that provide pregnancy-related benefits if they are issued on an expense-incurred basis. This applies to all policies covering residents who work within the state.

Massachusetts, in its general medical, surgical expense and blanket policies, provides the same level of infertility treatment as it does benefits for pregnancy-related procedures. Other regulations include infertility services in HMOs' preventive services. Insurers must provide benefits for all non-experimental infertility procedures and drugs, and have the option of covering experimental procedures, surrogacy and sterilization and reversal procedures.

Montana includes preventive and medically necessary infertility services in outpatient medical services.

New Mexico covers the diagnosis and treatment of physical conditions causing infertility – except for sterilization reversal – under basic health services.

New York mandates coverage of the diagnosis and treatment of correctable conditions that result in infertility.

Rhode Island mandates that infertility treatment be covered the same as other pregnancy-related procedures.

Texas mandates that all insurers – including HMOs and self-insurers – that provide pregnancy-related benefits also provide benefits for IVF on an expense-incurred basis, subject to certain conditions.

APPENDIX E

The Court Order

This is a series of legal documents used in California to ascribe parental rights in gestational surrogacy situations, in which the genetic material of the prospective parents were used. Similar documents would be filed in the case of egg donation with gestational surrogacy. The forms would vary significantly with traditional surrogacy.

Complaint to Declare Existence of Maternity and Paternity

Plaintiffs (genetic parents' names) allege:

1. That plaintiffs are residents of (county, state).

2. That defendant is a resident of (county, state).

3. Plaintiffs (genetic parents' names) reside together as man and wife in (state).

4. That defendant (surrogate's name) became pregnant on or about (date) through a medical procedure known is "Ovum Implantation", in (state).

5. That the "ovum implantation" procedure involved surgical removal from plaintiff (genetic mother's name) of ova (or eggs) and the in vitro fertilization of the ova with the semen of plaintiff, (genetic father's name) resulting in the conception of Plaintiff's biological child. Upon several cell divisions, the fertilized ova were then

implanted into the uterus of defendant (surrogate's name).

6. That defendant (surrogate's husband's name) is and has been married to Defendant (surrogate's name) since (date); however, the child to be born to Defendant, is not the issue of their marriage nor the biological chid of either (name of surrogate's husband and surrogate).

7. That plaintiff (genetic father) is alleged as aforesaid, and is entitled to a declaration of his paternal rights, and to legal affirmation of his paternal responsibilities, financial and otherwise, over said child.

8. That plaintiff (genetic mother) is the biological mother of the child to be born to defendant (surrogate), and is entitled to a declaration of her maternal rights and legal affirmation of her maternal responsibilities, financial and otherwise, over said child.

Date and attorney's signature.

Verification

We are the plaintiffs in the above entitled action; We have read the foregoing complaint and know the contents thereof; and we certify the same is true of our own knowledge, except as to those matters which are therein stated upon our information or belief, and as to those matters, we believe them to be true.

We declare under penalty of perjury under the laws of the State of (state name) that the foregoing is true and correct.

Executed on (date) at (location)

signatures of genetic parents.

Declaration of (Attorney's name)

I, (name of attorney), do declare:

1. I am an attorney, duly licensed to practice law in the state of (state's name), I am the attorney of record for plaintiffs (genetic parents' names). I make this declaration on facts within my personal knowledge, and if called upon to do so, could and would competently testify to all of the following facts.

2. On or about (date) plaintiffs (genetic parents' names) entered into an agreement with defendant, (surrogate's name) whereby it was agreed that Defendant (surrogate's name) would conceive a child by a method known as "ovum Implantation".

3. The ovum implantation procedure involved the surgical removal from Plaintiff (genetic mother) of ova, and the in vitro fertilization of the ova with the semen of Plaintiff (genetic father) resulting in the conception of plaintiffs' biological child. Upon several cell divisions, the fertilized ova were then implanted into the uterus of defendant (surrogate's name).

4. On or about (date), defendant (surrogate) was confirmed pregnant, and is due to deliver the child on or about (due date).

5. Pursuant to section 7006 of the Uniform Parentage Act, an action may be brought before the birth of the child (or children) to determine paternity. Equal protection principles would require that action for maternity be allowed to commence as well.

6. All parties have stipulated to Judgment in this matter. Please see Stipulation attached herein.

7. Defendant, (surrogate) is married and was married at the time of conception to (surrogate's husband's name)

and the unborn child is not the issue of this marriage of Defendant.

8. Plaintiff (genetic father) is the biological father of the child to be born to Defendant (surrogate) as alleged aforesaid, and is entitled to a declaration of his parental rights and legal affirmations of his paternal responsibilities, financial and otherwise, over said child.

9. Plaintiff (genetic mother) is the biological mother of the child to be born to defendant (surrogate's name) and is entitled to a declaration of her maternal rights and legal affirmation of her maternal responsibilities, financial and otherwise, over said child.

I declare under penalty of perjury under the laws of the state of (state name) that the foregoing is true and correct.

Executed this ___ day of (month and year) at (city, state).

Attorney's signature

Declaration of (infertility specialist)

I (physician's name), M.D. declare:

1. I am a physician, duly licensed to practice medicine in the state of _____. My specialties are (infertility, obstetrics and gynecology).

2. On or about (date), I implanted (surrogate's name) with the fertilized embryos of (genetic parents' names). A pregnancy was confirmed on or about (date) and a child is expected to be born on or about (due date).

3. I hereby acknowledge that the child to be born on or about (due date) to (surrogate) are the result of the implantation of the fertilized embryos of (genetic parents' names).

I declare under penalty of perjury under the laws of the state of _____ that the foregoing is true and correct.

Date and signature of the infertility specialist.

Stipulation for Entry of Judgment

It is hereby stipulated and agreed by and between Plaintiffs (names of genetic parents) and defendants (surrogate and her husband) that judgment be entered in favor of Plaintiffs and against Defendants, to have Plaintiffs declared to be the natural, biological and legal father and mother of the unborn child (genetic parents' last name); that Plaintiffs be granted custody as soon after birth as medical considerations allow; and that the parties hereto acknowledge and agree that they are informed of their rights under the Minimum Child Support Standards Act, that they make this agreement freely without threat of duress, and that the needs of the child will be adequately met under this agreement; and that the right to support of the child has not been assigned to any county program, and that no application for public assistance is pending.

Signatures of the genetic parents and their attorney and of the surrogate, her husband, and their attorney are on this document.

Judgment of Maternity and Paternity

Pursuant to the stipulation on file here, it is hereby adjudged, ordered an decreed as follows:

1. That Plaintiff (genetic father) have judgment against Defendant (surrogate), in that Plaintiff (genetic father) is declared to be the natural, biological, and legal father

of unborn child (genetic parents' last name).

2. That Plaintiff (genetic mother) have judgment against Defendant (surrogate), in that Plaintiff be declared to be the natural, biological, and legal mother of unborn child (genetic parents' last name).

3. That custody to said unborn child be awarded to Plaintiffs as soon after birth as medical considerations allow.

4. That financial responsibility for said unborn child shall rest solely with the Father (genetic father's name) and with the Mother (genetic mother's name).

5. That the Court hereby orders the attending physician responsible for delivering unborn child (insert genetic parents' last name) to enter the true and correct name of said child; and that (genetic father's name) shall be listed as the father, and that (genetic mother's name) shall be listed as the mother on the birth certificate of the child to be born of the ovum implantation herein, as the legal and natural parents of unborn child (genetic parents' last name).

APPENDIX F
Fertility Related Medicines

Clomiphene citrate is a follicle stimulating drug, introduced in the 1950s.

Contraindications (Symptoms or conditions for which use of this drug is discouraged):
- Liver disease.
- Ovarian cysts.
- Pregnancy.

Adverse reactions:
- Blurred vision.
- Ovarian cysts.
- Ovarian enlargement.
- Throbbing.
- Hot flashes.
- Insomnia.
- Irritability.

Gonadoptropin is the generic term for **Pergonal** and **Metrodin**. It stimulates follicle formation and maturation. Both

Pergonal and Metrodin must be reconstituted with sodium chloride immediately before they are injected.

Contraindications:
- High levels of follicle stimulating hormone, indicating primary ovarian failure.
- Uncontrolled thyroid or adrenal dysfunction.
- Organic intracranial lesions.
- Abnormal bleeding of undetermined origin.
- Ovarian cysts or enlargement not due to polycystic ovarian syndrome.
- Prior hypersensitivity to urofollitropin.
- Pregnancy.
- Certain types of infertility unless the patient is an IVF candidate.

Adverse reactions:
- Pulmonary and vascular complications.
- Ovarian hyperstimulation.
- Adnexal torsion.
- Ovarian enlargement.
- Abdominal pain.
- Sensitivity to either Metrodin or Pergonal, resulting in chills, musculoskeletal aches, joint pain, malaise, headache and fatigue.
- Ovarian cysts.
- Nausea, vomiting, diarrhea, abdominal cramps and bloating.

- Pain, rash, swelling and/or irritation at the injection site.
- Hemoperitoneum.
- Ectopic pregnancy.
- Congenital abnormalities.
- Body rashes.

Additionally, Metrodin also may cause:
- Dry skin.
- Hair loss.
- Hives.
- Breast tenderness.

Pergonal, in addition to the symptoms shared with Metrodin, also may cause:
- Dizziness.
- Tachycardia (excessively rapid heartbeats).
- Dyspnea (labored breathing).
- Tachypnea (excessively rapid respiration).

Lupron is used for advanced prostatic cancer. It also increases the circulatory levels of luteninizing hormone and follicle stimulating hormones. Levels drop to post-menopausal levels, however, after two to four weeks of use.

Contraindications:
- Anaphylactic reaction (exaggerated allergic reactions).

- Pregnancy.

Adverse reactions:
- Congestive heart failure.
- ECG changes/ischemia (poor blood flow to a specific area of the body).
- High blood pressure.
- Heart murmurs.
- Peripheral edema or pain.
- Hot flashes.
- Impotence.
- Anemia.
- Bone pain.
- Myalgia (muscle pain).
- Dizziness.
- General pain.
- Headache.
- Insomnia/sleep disorders.
- Dyspnea (labored breathing).
- Sinus congestion.
- Dermatitis.
- Changes in the frequency or urgency to urinate.
- Hematuriam (blood in the urine).
- Urinary tract infection.
- Asthenia (weakness).

Norethindrone is the generic name for Aygestin, which is used to suppress ovulation.

Contraindications:
- Blood clot disorders.
- Breast cancer.
- Undiagnosed abnormal vaginal bleeding.
- Pregnancy.

Adverse reactions:
- Nausea.
- Vomiting.
- Depression.
- High blood pressure.
- Dizziness.
- Lethargy.
- Blood clots.
- Swelling.
- Bloating.
- Abdominal cramps.
- Breakthrough bleeding.
- Altered menstrual flow.
- Painful or absent menstruation.
- Enlargement of benign tumors of the uterus.
- Cervical erosion.

- Abnormal secretions and vaginal candidiasis.
- Jaundice.
- High blood sugar.
- Dark spots on skin.
- Breast tenderness, enlargement and secretions.
- Decreased libido.

HCG is the generic term for **Profasi**, which is used to induce ovulation. Before use, it must be reconstituted with bacteriostatic water.

Contraindications are:
- Prostatic carcinoma.
- Androgen-dependent neoplasm.
- Prior allergic reactions to HCG.

Adverse reactions are:
- Headache.
- Irritability.
- Restlessness.
- Depression.
- Fatigue.
- Edema.
- Pain at the injection site.
- Local and systemic hypersensitivity.

APPENDIX G
Glossary

Amniocentesis: A medical test that obtains a sample of amniotic fluid from the amniotic sac in the uterus, to test for genetic defects or obstetrical complications.

Apnea: A temporary cessation of breathing.

Artificial insemination: The sperm of the intended father inseminates the surrogate, usually in a physician's office. There is no physical contact between the two during. The surrogate is the genetic mother as well as the birth mother.

Aspiration: Suction used to remove body fluids and, in this case, the eggs in fluid.

Blastocyst: The stage at which a fertilized egg has a central cavity surrounded by an outer cellular layer.

Blastomer: A cell produced during cleavage.

Capacitation: A process that removes the cap-like covering of sperm, which is necessary before they can fertilize an egg.

Carcinoma: Cancer.

Catheter: a tube to drain fluid from the body.

Cervix: The neck-like, lower end of the uterus.

Cesarean section: An operation by which a baby is taken from the uterus, by cutting through the walls of the abdomen and uterus.

Chromosomes: Chromosomes carry the genes. There are 23 pairs in humans.

Chromosomal abnormalities: Alterations in the genetic code that may cause a person to be more likely to develop specific diseases or conditions.

Clinical pregnancy: Pregnancies that would have been unnoticed under normal circumstances but that were identified as a direct result of the frequent and thorough testing of IVF centers.

Congenital: Pertaining to a condition present a birth, regardless of whether it was inherited or caused by the uterine environment.

Contractions: Changes in the muscles that cause them to become shortened and stiffened. Contractions occur as one of the final stages before birth.

Court order: The body of legal documents necessary in some states to declare the genetic parents the legal parents of their surrogate-born child.

CPR: Cardiopulmonary resuscitation, which is a procedure for reviving heart and lung functions.

Cryobank: A facility that stores frozen embryos or other frozen tissue.

Cryopreservation: A method of preserving pre-embryos that involves dehydration and storage at sub-zero temperatures for later resuscitation.

Cytoplasm: The substance between the cell wall and the cell nucleus.

Ejaculation: The sudden discharge of semen from the male reproductive tract.

Embryo: A mammal in the early stages of development within the womb. In humans, embryos are younger than two months.

Embryo implantation: The process of introducing an embryo into a womb.

Endometriosis: A condition in which the uterine lining, the endometrium, appears in the ovaries or other pelvic organs.

Epididymal: Having to do with the epididymis, the beginning of the vas deferens section of the testes.

Episiotomy: A surgical incision into the vagina and perineum to allow enough room for birth.

Estrogen: Female sex hormones. They are produced primarily by ovarian follicles.

Fertility specialist: A physician with advanced medical training or experience in human infertility.

Fetus: A mammal in the later stages of development in the womb. In humans, an embryo becomes a fetus at two months.

Follicle: Small sacs in the ovaries that contain unripened eggs.

Follicular fluid: Fluid contained within the follicles. It is aspirated with the eggs.

Geneticist: A person specially trained in genetics. Regarding pregnancy, this person discusses genetic diseases and the probability that they will appear in the child.

Gamete: A mature sperm or mature egg.

Genital tract: Reproductive tract.

Gestational surrogate: A woman who carries the child of another couple throughout the gestation period. The child has no genetic relationship to her.

Gynecologist: A physician who specializes in the health and diseases of women, especially the reproductive tract.

HCG: See human chorionic gonadotropin.

Higher order multiples: Triplets and other multiple births of greater numbers.

Human chorionic gonadotropin: HCG. A hormone that stimulates the production of estrogen and progesterone and causes the eggs to release from the follicle.

Hydrocephalus: An accumulation of serous fluid in the cranium that causes a great enlargement of the head. It also is known as "water on the brain."

Hyperstimulation: Over stimulation. In regards to ovarian stimulation, this causes the ovaries to produce and ripen multiple eggs simultaneously.

Hysterectomy: A surgery that removes a woman's uterus. Ovaries may be left intact.

ICU: Intensive care unit.

Immunologic: Having to do with the immune system.

Incubator: A device in which media (such as a sperm and egg mixture) are cultivated at a constant temperature, and in which premature infants are kept in a controlled environment to further their development.

Inseminate: To inject with semen.

Intrapartal: This refers to the birthing process.

Intravenous: Through the veins.

In uterine: In the uterus.

In vitro fertilization: Literally, fertilization in glass. The sperm and eggs of the intended parents are united outside the body and the resulting embryo is transferred to the uterus of either the mom or a surrogate.

Isolettes: Incubators that help premature infants to continue to develop.

IVF: In vitro fertilization.

Lamaze method: A method of preparing a woman for childbirth that emphasizes breathing exercises, psychological and physical conditioning.

Laproscopic surgery: Surgery that is performed using a fiberoptic instrument called a laproscope. It is equipped with a camera, scissors and other instruments and is inserted through a small incision.

Lutenizing hormone: A hormone released by the pituitary gland that stimulates the maturation of the ovarian follicle.

Maternity benefits: Those benefits covered under health insurance that are directly related to pregnancy. They typically include prenatal care, hospitalization and delivery, but may vary according to the policy.

Menopause: The time when menstruation stops permanently, usually between ages 45 and 55.

Neonatal: Pertaining to newborn children.

Nucleus: A specialized, usually spherical mass of protoplasm that directs cell growth, reproduction, metabolism and the functioning of genetic characteristics.

Oocyte: An immature egg cell.

Osmosis: The movement of fluid through a semipermeable membrane, such as the cell wall.

Outpatient procedure: A medical procedure that is performed in a clinic or hospital but that does not require an overnight stay.

Ovaries: Female reproductive glands.

Ovum: The female reproductive cell that, after fertilization, can developed into a new individual.

PAP smear: A medical test for cancer of the cervix.

Paracervical block: An anesthesia that blocks pain across the cervix. Also called a saddle block.

Patient Advocate: A hospital employee, usually in the social services department, who works with the patient or family to explain or streamline hospital procedures and paperwork, including resolving such issues as birth certificates, visiting rights, insurance claims, hospital cash discounts, etc.

Permeability: The ability of liquids, such as cryoprotectants, to enter the pre-embryos.

Pipette: A slender, graduated tube used in laboratories to measure and transfer quantities of liquid between or among containers.

Placenta: An organ within the uterus that provides the nourishment and helps eliminate waste products from a developing mammal.

Postpartal: The period after a child's birth.

Potassium chloride: A water soluble chemical used in the production of fertilizers. When injected into a fetus, it causes instant death and, therefore, is used for selective termination.

Percutaneous: Through the skin.

Pre-embryo: A term applied to the fertilized egg the first few days after fertilization before it becomes a blastocyst and before the fertilized egg attaches to the uterine wall.

Pre-existing condition: For insurance purposes, a medical condition that already exists in the person to be covered. Such conditions may not be covered by some policies, or may be cause to exclude the person from any coverage under a given policy.

Prenatal: Before birth.

Procreation: The process of producing offspring.

Progesterone: A hormone that prepares the uterus for the fertilized ovum and maintains pregnancy.

Pronuclei: The nuclei of the sperm and egg just before they form one nucleus.

Seeding: A step in cryopreservation in which "seeds" of ice are created by touching straw containing the pre-embryos with a pair of super-cooled tweezers. This allows the freezing process to be controlled.

Selective reduction: A medical procedure in which an embryo is removed from the womb in an effort to allow the remaining embryos to survive or to enhance the safety of the pregnancy for the woman.

Semen: The fluid produced by the male reproductive system, which contains the sperm.

Singletons: Babies born singly, rather than as twins or higher order multiples.

Societal concern: That which concerns society as a whole, rather than only the individuals involved. IVF and surrogacy both are considered societal concerns because of their affect upon what we, as a society, allow ourselves to become.

Sperm: Male reproductive cells within the semen.

Straw: A tube that holds cryopreserved embryos, typically four per straw.

Surrogate: A person who acts in place of another. In surrogate parenthood, a surrogate would act for the mother by carrying the child and delivering it.

Teflon: A brand of polytetrafluorethylene used as coating to create smooth, non-stick surfaces. For IVF, it lines the catheter used to aspirate the eggs from the follicles.

Tertiary care unit: The third level of hospital care. This level requires specialized services and is more critical than primary or secondary levels of care, and may be called intensive care.

Testicle: The male reproductive gland.

Traditional surrogacy: Surrogacy in which the egg is contributed by the woman carrying the child and the sperm is provided via artificial insemination.

Trophoblastic: The cell layer that nourishes the embryo and develops into the placenta.

Ultrasound: Ultrasonic waves that are used to form pictures of the embryo or fetus inside the uterus.

Uterus: The womb, where the fertilized ovum implants and develops.

Vaginal: Pertaining to the vagina, which is the passage leading from the uterus to the vulva (the external female genitalia) of females.

Vas deferens: The tube that conducts sperm to the penis from the epididymis.

Vitrification: The process of turning fluid into a non-crystalline, glass-like solid.

Wastage: In relation to IVF, wastage refers to pre-embryos that are neither implanted nor cryopreserved.

Womb: The uterus.

Zona pellucida: The egg's outer shell.

Zygote: The cell produced by two gametes (sperm and egg) before it divides.

APPENDIX H
Bibliography

A State Model for Public Policy on Bioethics, The New York State Task Force on Life and Law, July 1994.

Aesoph, Lauri M.: "Coping With Male Infertility," Natural Healing, Web page, New Hope Communication, 1995.

After Baby M: The Legal, Ethical and Social Dimensions of Surrogacy, New Jersey Commission on Legal and Ethical Problems in the Delivery of Health Care, Trenton, NJ, 1992.

Aigen, Betsey: Motivations of Surrogate Mothers: Parenthood, Altruism and Self-Actualization.

Alternative Reproduction Act of 1992, State of California, SB 937.

Altieri, Domenica: "Commercial Surrogacy: Questions and Considerations of Parties with Vested Interests," Woodrow Wilson Biology Institute, 1992.

American Academy of Pediatrics Recommendations on Surrogate Motherhood Arrangements, 1992.

Andrews, Lori, Elster, Nanette: Surrogacy Law Chart, Illinois Institute of Technology, Chicago-Kent College of Law. 1996.

Arizona Revised Statutes 25-218.

"Assisted Reproductive Technology in the United States and Canada: 1994 Results Generated from the American

Society for Reproductive Medicine/Society for Assisted Reproductive Technology Registry," Fertility and Sterility, pp.697-705, Vol. 66, No. 5, November 1996.

Bonner, Denise, interview, August 1995.

Brinsden, Peter R. and Paul A. Rainsbury, (ed): A Textbook of In Vitro Fertilization and Assisted Reproduction, Parthenon Publishing Group, Park Ridge, N.J., pp 451, 1992.

Brophy, Katie: Surrogate Family Services, interview August 1992.

"Canada Seeks to Ban Surrogate Motherhood," Associated Press, June 15, 1996.

"Cardinal Backs Embryos' Demise," Associated Press, August 1, 1996.

Carter, Sandra: Infertility Center of America, interview, August 1992.

Ciccarelli, John K.: "Provisions a Surrogacy Contract Should Contain." Center for Surrogate Parenting & Egg Donation, Inc., Los Angeles, CA 1995.

Clapp, Diane N.: What is an Infertility Specialist. Resolve Web page 1996.

"Clomiphene Citrate" Bay Area Fertility Medical Group, Web page, 1995.

Collins, J.A., et al: "An Estimate of the Cost of In Vitro Fertilization Services in the United States in 1995," F&S, pp538-45 n.64, 1995.

Collins, Robert L.: Ovulation Induction, Springer-Verlag, New York, 1991.

Considerations and Implications for Couples, COTS Web page, 1996.

Considerations for Potential Surrogate Mothers, COTS Web page, 1996.

Cook, Carol: Centers for Disease Control, interview, July 1996.

Coughlan, Michael J.: The Vatican, the Law and the Human Embryo, University of Iowa Press, Iowa City, IA, pp1-7, 1990.

Corea, Gena: The Mother Machine: Reproductive Technologies from Artificial Insemination to Artificial Wombs, Harper & Row, New York, 1985.

Daniels, Ken: "Review of the New Zealand Government Report into Assisted Human Reproduction, Eubios Ethics Institute Newsletter 4, pp58-59, September 1994.

D.C. Code, Ann. 16-401.

Dolgin, Janet L.: "Status and Contract In Surrogate Motherhood: An Illumination of the Surrogacy Debate," Daily Journal Report, pp2-18, December 28, 1990.

Donati, Theresa: Farleigh Dickinson University, Society for the Scientific Study of Religion, interview, July 1995.

Drellow, Pam: Blue Cross Blue Shield Association, interview, July 1996.

Ebrahim, Abul Fadl Mohsin: Abortion, Birth Control and Surrogate Parenting: An Islamic Perspective, American Trust Publications, Indianapolis, 1989.

Efron, Sonni: "Bill to Legalize Surrogacy is Introduced," pp B1, Los Angeles Times, April 28, 1991.

Elster, Nanette: Illinois Institute of Technology, Chicago-Kent College of Law, interview, August 1996.

Ethical Issues in Surrogate Motherhood, American Academy of Pediatrics, Elk Grove Village, IL 1992.

Eubios News, v.215, pp 2-3, 1996.

"Family Ties: Desire Outweighs DNA," Science News, pp333, May 27, 1995.

"Fee Schedule," Saddleback Center for Reproductive Health, 1992.

Feinman, Clarice (ed).: The Criminalization of a Woman's Body, The Haworth Press, Inc., Binghamton, NY, pp. 221, 1992.

Ferguson, Mike: Self Insured Industry Association, interview July 1996.

First Meeting, COTS Web page, 1996.

Fisch, Harry: "Geographic Variability May Explain Why Earlier Researchers Reached Wrong Conclusions," Columbia-Presbyterian Medical Center, New York, NY, May 3, 1996.

Fisch, Harry: "Fluctuations in Birth Rates Tied to Fluctuations in Sperm Counts," American Urological Association meeting, May 6,1996.

Florida State Statutes 742.09-742.17

Gitlin, H. Joseph: interview, June 1995.

Gostin, Larry: Surrogate Motherhood: Politics and Privacy, Indiana University Press, Bloomington, 1990.

Greil, Arthur L., "The Religious Response to Reproductive Technology," The Christian Century, pp11-14, January 4-11, 1989.

Greil, Arthur L., interview, August 1995.

Goldenbery, Robert L. and Tsunenobu Tamura: "Pre-pregnancy Weight and Pregnancy Outcome," Journal of the American Medical Association, April 9, 1996.

Goldfarb, J.M. et al.: "Cost Effectiveness of In vitro Fertilization," Obstetrics & Gynecology, n. 87, pp18-21, 1996.

"Hormonal Clock Predicts Premature Births," Science News, pp260, vol.147, 1995.

"How to Enhance Your Fertility (and Help to Ensure a Healthier Baby, Too)," Rose Men's Health Resource, Web page, Rose Medical Center, 1993.

Hughes, J.J. and Keown, D: "Buddhism and Medical Ethics: A Bibliographic Introduction," Journal of Buddhist Ethics, 1995, http://www.JBE.com

Huntington Reproductive Seminar, infertility seminar, April 1996.

"In Vitro Fertilization and Uterine Embryo Transfer", Huntington Reproductive Center, Pasadena California, 1996.

Iglesias, Teresa: IVF and Justice. Linacre Centre for Health Care Ethics, London, 1990.

Indiana Code 31-8.

Iowa Code 710.11.

Jersild, Paul T.: In Vitro Fertilization, pp12, Division for Mission in North America, Lutheran Church in America, NY, 1986.

Judson, George: "The Trials of an American Midwife: She Fights to Keep Delivering Babies at Home – With Less Footing Than a Stork, She Fights to Deliver in the Home," New York Times, pp25, November 4, 1995.

Kamrava, Michael: West Coast Infertilty & Reproductive Associates, interview and personal communications, January 1997.

Karcher, Helmut L.: "Germany Bans Surrogacy," British Medical Journal, pp1063, 301(6760), November 10, 1990.

Kentucky Code Chapter 199, Section 590.

Khazoum, Judith L. Bellow: "The Ethics of Surrogate Motherhood," Dialog, vol 28, No 3.

Kieley, John, "Study Finds Large Increase in Multiple Births Among White Mothers," American Journal of Diseases of Children, July 1992.

Kristof, Kathy: "A New Wave of Tax Changes Nears," Los Angeles Times, pp D3, August 7, 1996.

Larson, Edward J.: "Personhood: Current Legal Views," Second Opinion, pp40-54, July 1990.

"Lasers Advance Infertility Treatment," UCI News, University of California at Irvine, September 30, 1992.

Macer, Darryl R..J.: "Perception of Risks and Benefits of In Vitro Fertilisation, Genetic Engineering and Biotechnology," Social Science and Medicine, pp 22-33, Vol. 38, 1994.

"Making the Sperm of Others," U.S. News & World Report, pp 19, June 10, 1996.

Marquis, Julie: "Fertility Procedure Controls Pass Easily in State Senate," Los Angeles Times, p5, August 21, 1996.

Martinez, Gebe: "Congress Logs On to Cyberspace," Los Angeles Times, p1, September 4, 1996.

"Maternal Obesity Doubles Risk for Birth Defects," Journal of the American Medical Association April 9, 1996.

McDowell, Janet Dickey: Surrogate Motherhood, Division for Mission in North America, Lutheran Church in America, NY, pp15, 1986.

McNeil, Mauree, Ian Varcoe and Steven Yearley (ed): The New Reproductive Technologies, Macmillan, London, 1990.

Montalbano, William D.: "Fertile Ground for Ethics Debate," Los Angeles Times, ppA2, August 10, 1996.

Montgomery, Cristie: Surrogate Parenting Services, interviews, July 1992 and November 1996.

Moseley, Norma: House Ways & Means Committee, interview, August 1996.

NAIC's Compendium of State Laws on Insurance Topics, National Association of Insurance Commissioners, 1996.

Nassor, Ali: "Surrogate Mothers Cash In," St. Petersburg Press, 1996, Russia, http://www.spb.su/sppress/104/surrogat.html.

New Jersey Parentage Act, New Jersey Permanent Statutes, 9:17-41.

New Reproductive Technologies, Calgary West Federal Liberal Association Web page, July 1995.

Newsletter, Center for Surrogate Parenting & Egg Donation, Inc., vol. 1. No. 5, 1994.

Nilsson, Lennart and Hamberger, Lars: A Child is Born, Delacorte Press/Seymour Lawrence, Bantam Doubleday Dell Publishing Group, Inc., New York, 1990.

Ng, S.C. Bongso, T.A. and Ratnam, S.S. , "Micro-insemination: genetic aspects," Archives of Adrology, 1991.

"Opinions on Confidentiality, Advertising, and Communications Media Relations" American Medical Association, June 1996.

Opsahl, Michael: Genetics & IVF Institute, interview, September 1996.

Organization of Parents Through Surrogacy, Web Page, 1996.

"Ovary Cryopreservation," Genetics & IVF Institute Web page.

"Overview of Laws and Legal Precedents Affecting Surrogate Arrangements," ECHOS Web page, 1996.

Overvold, Amy Zuckerman: Surrogate Parenting, Ballantine Books, New York, 1988.

Oz, Shlomit Joy: Genetic Mother vs. Surrogate Mother: Which Does the Law Recognize? A Comparison of Jewish Law, American Law, and England's Law. Web page, 1996.

"Pergonal and Metrodin," Bay Area Fertility Medical Group, Web page, 1995.

Perloe, Mark and Cristie, Linda Gail: "Maximizing Male Fertility Potential," Miracle Babies and Other Happy Endings for Couples with Fertility Problems. Mark Perloe, M.D., P.C. Atlanta, GA. Web page, 1995.

Physicians' Desk Reference. Medical Economics Data Products Co., Montvale, NJ 1996.

Pope: Gregory T: "Brave New World," Popular Mechanics, pp88-89, February 1994.

Rae, Scott B.: The Ethics of Commercial Surrogate Motherhood: Brave New Families? Praeger, Westport, CT, 1994.

Ragone Helena: Surrogate Motherhood: Conception in the Heart, Westview Press, Boulder, CO, pp 215, 1994.

Rahimomran, Abdel: Family Planning in the Legacy of Islam, Routledge, New York, pp. 284, 1992.

"Religious Perspectives," Infertility: Medical and Social Choices, U.S. Congress, Office of Technology Assessment, Government Printing Office, Washington, D.C., 1988.

Roan, Shari: "How Many Babies is Too Many?" Los Angeles Times, pp1, May 14, 1996.

Robertson, John A., Children of Choice: Freedom and the New Reproductive Technologies, Princeton University Press, Princeton, N.J., pp 281, 1994.

Salome, Louis J., "Surrogate Mom Carries a Grandchild," The Atlanta Journal/The Atlanta Constitution, April 28, 1996.

Sanpere, Alice: The Practice of Nurse-Midwifery, Web page, August 1996.

Sauer, Mark V. RJ Paulson, R.A. Lobo: "A Preliminary Report on Oocyte Donation Extending Reproductive Potential to Women over 40," New England Journal of Medicine, pp1157-1160, vol. 323, no. 17, October 25, 1990.

Schneider, Edward D.: Artificial Insemination, pp16, Division for Mission in North America, Lutheran Church in America, NY, 1986.

Serafini, Paulo, J. Nelson, C. Tran, T. Tan, J. Batzofin: Assisted Reproductive Treatments: Patient Selection, Workup, Indications and Results, Huntington Reproductive Center, Pasadena, CA, 1996.

Shabanowitz, Robert: "Embryo Cryopreservation," Geisinger Medical Center's Fertility Center, Web Page, August, 1996.

Shannon, Thomas A.: Surrogate Motherhood: The Ethics of Using Human Beings, Crossroad Publishing Company, New York, pp.191, 1988.

Shaw, RW (ed): Assisted Reproduction: Progress in Research and Practice, the Parthenon Publishing Group, New York and Lancs, Britain, 1995.

Shibate, Henry, Buddhist Churches of America, interview, July 1995.

Shirai, Yasuko: "What Future for Surrogacy in Japan?" Eubios Ethics Institute Newsletter, pp3. No. 3, 1993.

Sloan, Gale A.: Postponing Parenthood: The Effect of Age on Reproductive Potential, Plenum Publishing Corporation, New York, pp 286, 1993.

Smith, Harmon L., and Lewis, Paul A.: "A Protestant View of the New Reproductive Technologies," Second Opinion, pp94-9-105, July 1990.

Stargot, Ilene: NINE, interview July 1995.

Sugarman, Mitchell: Kaiser Permanente, interview, July 1996.

Surrogacy Legislation, The Organization of Parents Through Surrogacy, 1996.

Surrogate Applicant Questionnaire, COTS Web page, 1996.

Surrogate Motherhood Policy, Medical Association of South Africa, Web page, 1996.

"Making the Sperm of Others", U.S. News and World Report, pp19, June 10, 1996.

Texas Family Code, Sec. 12.01-12.03

Vines, Gail: "Deep Freeze Leaves Its Mark on Mice," New Scientist, pp14-15, February 4, 1995.

Virginia Code 20-156-165

Virginia Code Ann. 54.1-7.1

Wallace, Meg: Surrogacy, Australian Capital Territory, Canberra, 1993.

Wartik, Nancy: "Making Babies," Los Angeles Times Magazine, pp18, March 6, 1994.

Weber, T, and Berkman, L: "Inquiries Target Fertility Clinic at UC Irvine", Los Angeles Times, ppA1, May 20, 1995.

Weber, T and Michael Granberry: "Babies are Bottom Line for Clinics," Los Angeles Times, pp A1, May 23, 1995.

"What's Your Success Rate?" Genetics & IVF Institute, Web page, 1996.

Wilson, Pete: Memo to the California Senate regarding SB937, September 26, 1992.

Winter, Ruth: A Consumer's Dictionary of Medicines. pp334, Crown Trade Paperbacks, New York, 1993.

Wood, Carl, Alan. Trounson: Clinical In Vitro Fertilization, Springer Verlag, New York, 1989.

Wyckoff, Kathy: Center for Reproductive Alternatives, interview, November 1991.

Zivari, Pamela: Baha'is of the United States, interview, September 1996.

Index

accidental loss, 77
accreditation, 84
adoption, 11, 44, 45, 56, 59, 60, 61, 62, 65, 69, 70, 71, 78, 79, 102, 117, 155
Adventist, 51
Alabama, 62
American Society of Reproductive Medicine, 22, 90, 181, 183
amniocentesis, 118, 126, 134, 157, 158, 160
Anglican, 51
Arizona, 62, 189
Arkansas, 62
artificial insemination, 11, 52, 71, 79, 210
Aspiration, 8, 28, 38, 203
Australia, 36, 40, 77, 221
Baha'i, 52, 221
Baptist, 51
blastocyst, 24, 48
blastomer, 24
boundaries, 162
breast feed, 162, 168
Buddhist, 52, 215, 220
California, 58. *See* law
Canada, 77, 78, 212
capacitation, 18
catheter, 19, 20, 210
Catholic, 50, 51, 53, 96
Children, 11, 27, 96, 105, 166, 216, 219
children, disclosing surrogacy, 108
Christian, 51, 54, 102, 215
Christian Scientist, 51
chromosomal abnormalities, 19
Clomiphene citrate, 197
clinical pregnancy, 85
Closed programs, 117
communicable diseases, 128
Conservative Jewish, 51
contract, 1, 4, 7, 9, 44, 45, 56, 58, 61, 62, 63, 64, 68, 69, 70, 71, 75, 77, 80, 82, 104, 111, 116, 118, 130, 131, 132, 133, 134, 135, 140, 142, 144, 145, 157, 161, 163, 167, 169, 185, 190
Contracts, 130, 133

Index A Matter of Trust : The Guide to Gestational Surrogacy

Costs, 90, 139
counseling, 58, 69, 112, 116, 131, 133, 136, 173
court, 5, 11, 59, 61, 62, 64, 69, 71, 84, 112, 149, 152, 153, 154
court order, 5, 11, 62, 112, 149, 152, 153, 154
cryobank, 7
Cryopreservation, 23, 25, 40, 46, 205, 218, 220
delivery, 138
Demographics, 95
Denmark, 78
Dietitian, 138
distance, 156
District of Columbia, 63
division of authority, 161
egg donors, 86
Embryo Ownership, 76
emotional support, 117, 129, 131, 159
ethics, 42, 52, 211
Evangelical, 51
expectations, 91, 118, 123, 127, 128
expenses, 9, 15, 37, 45, 46, 59, 61, 64, 66, 68, 69, 70, 74, 82, 103, 105, 111, 114, 123, 128, 131, 132, 135, 137, 138, 139, 140, 142, 145, 151, 158, 167, 190, 191
family law, 59, 61
fertility clinics, 7, 53, 84, 86, 90, 91
finances, 37, 46, 137
first meeting, 124, 162
Florida, 64, 65, 190, 214
France, 78
friends as surrogates, 120
Georgia, 65, 216
Germany, 78, 216
gonadoptropin, 15
goodbye, 169
Great Britain, 40, 50, 53, 79
HCG, 8, 15, 17, 85, 202, 206
Health insurance, 138
Home Births, 150
hospital, 3, 4, 5, 6, 9, 36, 37, 66, 70, 88, 92, 134, 143, 144, 145, 146, 147, 148, 149, 150, 151, 153, 154, 164, 169, 170, 171, 190, 207, 208, 210
Illinois, 48, 65, 190, 212, 214
implantation, 2, 7, 23, 26, 27, 29, 48, 85, 111, 140, 161, 163, 166, 192, 193, 195, 196, 205
implantation restrictions, 76
Indiana, 66, 97, 187, 214, 215
infertility clinics, 7, 84, 90
infertility statistics, 96
International Laws, 77
Iowa, 67, 213

Index A Matter of Trust : The Guide to Gestational Surrogacy

Islam, 54, 214, 219
Israel, 80
IVF, 12, 27, 29, 30, 32, 35, 37, 38, 40, 42, 43, 49, 50, 51, 53, 56, 74, 78, 83, 87, 88, 89, 90, 105, 139, 141, 168, 182, 189, 190, 191, 198, 204, 207, 209, 210, 215, 218, 221. *See* in vitro fertilization
Japan, 23, 42, 80, 220
Jehovah's Witness, 51
Jewish, 50, 51, 54, 55, 56, 80, 218
Johnson vs. Calvert, 58
Kentucky, 68
laproscopic surgery, 40
Life insurance, 136, 138
Louisiana, 48
Lutheran, 50, 51, 53, 216, 217, 219
Maine, 68
Maternity coverage, 142
medical testing, 128
Medications, 138, 139
Mennonite, 51
Methodist, 51
Metrodin, 15, 16, 198, 199, 218
Michigan, 45, 68
Microhatching, 91
midwife, 150, 151, 152
minimum wage law, 59
Minnesota, 48, 68, 128
Misconduct, 84
Mormon, 51
Muslim, 51
Nebraska, 69
Nevada, 69
New Hampshire, 69
New Jersey, 61, 70, 211
New York, 32, 33, 35, 45, 70, 97, 103, 191, 211, 213, 214, 216, 218, 219, 220, 221
New Zealand, 42, 43, 81, 213
Norlutate, 8, 201
North Dakota, 70
obstetricians, 112, 146, 151
open programs, 117
Orthodox Jewish, 51
Pager, 138
patient advocate, 5, 147, 149
Pergonal, 8, 15, 16, 198, 199, 218
Personality Profile, 118
personhood, 48, 52, 58
potassium chloride, 21

Index   A Matter of Trust : The Guide to Gestational Surrogacy

pre-embryo, 2, 7, 12, 19, 24, 25, 28, 38, 42, 47, 48, 49, 55, 65, 77, 78, 85, 161, 205, 208, 209, 211
progesterone, 17, 206
psychological screening, 69, 104, 136
psychologist, 102, 104, 110, 112, 128, 129, 136
Psychotherapist, 132
reassurance, 167, 171, 172
Reform Jewish, 51
relatives as surrogates, 120
Resolve, 90, 184, 213
rumors, 164
Russia, 81, 217
seeding, 25, 209
selective reduction, 21, 118, 120, 134
South Africa, 82, 220
Success Rates, 29, 85
Support groups, 168
surrogacy agreement, 8, 61, 63, 67, 69, 74, 75, 79, 81, 109, 111, 131, 132, 136, 153, 158
surrogate, 1, 2, 3, 4, 5, 6, 7, 8, 9, 11, 12, 13, 17, 21, 22, 29, 30, 42, 44, 45, 46, 50, 51, 53, 54, 55, 56, 58, 59, 60, 61, 62, 63, 64, 67, 68, 69, 70, 71, 74, 75, 80, 81, 82, 86, 87, 88, 89, 92, 95, 96, 97, 102, 103, 104, 105, 108, 109, 110, 111, 112, 113, 114, 115, 116, 117, 118, 120, 121, 122, 123, 124, 125, 126, 127, 128, 129, 130, 131, 132, 133, 134, 135, 136, 137, 138, 139, 140, 141, 142, 143, 144, 145, 146, 147, 148, 149, 150, 151, 152, 153, 154, 155, 156, 157, 158, 159, 160, 161, 162, 163, 164, 165, 166, 167, 168, 169, 170, 171, 172, 173, 175, 176, 186, 188, 192, 193, 194, 195, 196, 203, 204, 206, 207, 210
surrogate demographics, 97
Switzerland, 83
Tennessee, 71
tertiary care, 4, 143
Texas, 71, 191, 221
the Organization of Parents Through Surrogacy, 11, 61, 90, 113, 185
traditional surrogacy, 11, 43, 51, 68, 74, 147, 191
treatment, 1, 3, 9, 12, 23, 35, 39, 40, 42, 43, 45, 50, 54, 56, 57, 59, 64, 74, 78, 81, 86, 87, 88, 89, 90, 91, 93, 94, 95, 137, 139, 141, 142, 145, 147, 164, 189, 190, 191, 219
U.S. state law, 3, 45, 52, 54, 55, 56, 58, 59, 60, 61, 62, 63, 65, 66, 68, 69, 70, 74, 77, 78, 79, 80, 81, 88, 112, 114, 117, 121, 128, 130, 132, 134, 135, 136, 144, 150, 151, 152, 153, 154, 157, 164, 176, 193, 194, 195
ultrasound, 9, 13, 16, 17, 18, 85, 91, 139, 157, 163, 168
Utah, 45, 71
Vatican, 57, 213
Virginia, 40, 45, 71, 74, 75, 221
vitrification, 25
Washington, 74, 75, 183, 219
wastage, 42, 51, 211

Index   A Matter of Trust : The Guide to Gestational Surrogacy

weight, 5, 15, 27, 36, 121, 123, 177
West Virginia, 74
wills, 2, 111, 135, 138, 140
zygote, 19, 55, 63

Order Form

Fax orders: 1-714-726-9094
Phone orders: 1-714-786-4606
Postal orders: Clouds Publishing
                 5319 University Drive, #348
                 Irvine, CA 92612-2935

Please send ____ copies of **A Matter of Trust: The Guide to Gestational Surrogacy**

Name:_____

Mailing Address:_____

City:_____ State:_____ ZIP:_____

Daytime Phone:_____

Price: $21.95 U.S.
CA residents add 7.75% sales tax   _____
Shipping: $6.25 for two day U.S. service,
(up to 4 books, shipped Airborne Express   _____

Total: $_____
Payment:
Check enclosed____; Credit card: MasterCard __ Visa__
Card number:_____
Expiration date:_____

Name on card:_____

Signature:_____

Order Form

Fax orders: 1-714-726-9094
Phone orders: 1-714-786-4606
Postal orders: Clouds Publishing
         5319 University Drive, #348
         Irvine, CA 92612-2935

Please send ____ copies of **A Matter of Trust: The Guide to Gestational Surrogacy**

Name:_____

Mailing Address:_____

City:_____ State:_____ ZIP:_____

Daytime Phone:_____

Price: $21.95 U.S.
CA residents add 7.75% sales tax   _____
Shipping: $6.25 for two day U.S. service,
(up to 4 books, shipped Airborne Express _____

Total: $_____
Payment:
Check enclosed____; Credit card: MasterCard __ Visa__
Card number:_____
Expiration date:_____

Name on card:_____

Signature:_____